ICT AND LITERACY

Also available from Continuum:

Avril Loveless: *The Role of IT: Practical Issues for the Primary Teacher*
Manjula Datta (ed.): *Bilinguality and Literacy*
Andrew Goodwyn (ed.): *English in the Digital Age*
Duncan Grey: *The Internet in School* (Second Edition)
Jon Griffin and Leslie Bash (eds): *Computers in the Primary School*
Diane Montgomery: *Spelling*
Adrian Oldknow and Ron Taylor: *Teaching Maths with ICT*
Lez Smart: *Using IT in Primary School History*
Keith Topping: *Paired Reading, Spelling and Writing*

ICT and Literacy
Information and Communications Technology, Media, Reading and Writing

Edited by
Nikki Gamble and Nick Easingwood

CONTINUUM
London and New York

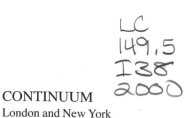

Continuum
The Tower Building
11 York Road
London SE1 7NX

370 Lexington Avenue
New York
NY 10017–6503

First published 2000

British Library Cataloguing-in-Publication Data
A catalogue record for this book is available from the British Library.

ISBN   0–8264–4810–0

Typeset by Kenneth Burnley, Wirral, Cheshire.
Printed and bound in Great Britain by TJ International Ltd, Padstow, Cornwall.

Contents

Part Three: Professional Issues

Contributors

Nikki Gamble is Senior Lecturer in English in the School of Education at Anglia Polytechnic University, where she teaches on the Primary undergraduate and PGCE programmes and on in-service Master's degree courses. Nikki's main teaching and academic interests are in children's literature and reading development, and new literacies. She is a member of IRSCL (International Research Society in Children's Literature), secretary for BALCL (British Association of Lecturers in Children's Literature) and she serves on the committee of the British section of IBBY (International Board on Books for Young People).

Nick Easingwood is Senior Lecturer in ICT in Education at Anglia Polytechnic University. He joined the School of Education in September 1997 following eleven years as an Essex primary school teacher. He currently teaches ICT in the curriculum on the postgraduate and undergraduate Initial Teacher Education courses, as well as on in-service Master's degree courses. He maintains regular contact with schools through his work as a teacher trainer, in which he visits students on their school experiences.

Professor **Stephen Heppell** is director of Ultralab at Anglia Polytechnic University. The lab is 'Europe's foremost learning technology research centre' with a vast portfolio of major projects at the intersection of learning, technology and research, including the *Guinness Book of Records*' 'Largest Internet learning project in the world'. Ultralab projects pioneered CD-ROM technology in the 1980s, internet learning communities and communities of practice in the mid-1990s and, most recently, non-narrative new media authoring. New research is particularly focused on intelligent toys, third generation mobile phones and new digital media. Additionally, Stephen is a former teacher, a current parent and an obsessive dinghy sailor!

Sue Brindley is Lecturer in Education at the University of Cambridge, where she teaches Master's level courses and co-ordinates the English PGCE. She is currently researching into ICT use in schools, with a particular focus on literacy.

Angela McFarlane was appointed Professor of Education at the University of Bristol during 2000. Formerly Director for Evidence and Practice at BECTa, and Director of the Centre for Research in Educational ICT at Homerton College, Cambridge, she has a wealth of experience in research, teaching and writing concerning the use of ICT.

Grace Kempster is Head of Libraries, Information Heritage and Cultural Services for Essex County Council. Before joining Essex in 1996, she spent three years transforming the library and information service in Leeds where she established the online@leeds project for children in schools and libraries, set up an award-winning website for the city and started the innovative Leeds Word Arena project. A passionate champion of children and reading – and readers – she is a commissioner on the Library and Information Commission and was closely involved in the seminal report *New Library: The People's Network,* and led the task group that advised on ICT training for library staff.

Richard Millwood is a Reader in Educational Technology at Ultralab, Anglia Polytechnic University's laboratory that researches and develops the use of information technology in learning. His work involves initiating research and development projects, preparing proposals for their funding and the subsequent management of a multidisciplinary, and sometimes geographically dispersed, development team. He makes regular contributions to international conferences in the field of educational computing and is frequently in demand as a consultant to a number of educational and computing organizations.

Rebecca James is an English teacher and writer living in East Sussex. She started to research CD-ROMs while studying for an MA in Children's Literature at the University of Surrey Roehampton. Her other research interests include the differences between girls' and boys' experience of learning and spiritual values in teenage fiction.

Sarah Mears is a librarian who believes passionately in the power of libraries to change lives. Sarah has spent most of her working life with Essex Libraries but also worked for Redbridge Libraries. Sarah is currently working with Essex LEA as Study Support Manager, producing a strategy to develop out-of-school-hours learning within the county.

Marilyn Foreman has been Senior Lecturer for English in the School of Education at Anglia Polytechnic University since 1998, following an extensive teaching career which culminated in a deputy headship of a large Essex primary school. Her main interests include children's writing, especially concerning the use of new technologies, and she teaches on the Primary undergraduate and PGCE programmes.

Angela McGlashon is a Senior Lecturer for mPowernet, Anglia Polytechnic University's New Opportunity Fund's department for training teachers in schools. In addition to being a tutor, she has also been a tutor at Anglia Polytechnic University's School of Education where she taught on the Primary undergraduate programmes. This followed many years' experience as a teacher in a variety of schools in Essex and Redbridge, as well as being a teacher with the Essex Special Needs Support Service where she was ICT Coordinator/ Adviser for children with statements. She is also a past member of Essex National Grid for Learning steering group.

Foreword

Do the new technologies of computers, mobile phones, the Internet, games consoles, wireless pocket organizers and ubiquitous digital television herald the disappearance of the literate child or the beginning of an era of new broader literacy? It depends, of course, on your perspective and this book seeks to inform that perspective.

It seems that as each generation of children bumps up against a new technology, two things happen simultaneously. First, the children conquer and harness that new technology in a quite exhilarating way while, second, their teachers and parents express alarm at the damage that the mythology of the day suggests will result. Adults enjoy but a brief skirmish with the new devices while prices remain at a premium but then, as prices tumble, the kids take over and culture shifts, often significantly. We have so many examples to look back at: adults feared for the hearing of adolescents whose ears were pressed tight against the first 'transistor radios', while new radio stations had to be rapidly and, often illegally, created to meet their needs. A couple of decades later, after a brief existence as adult entertainment in pubs, computer games quickly decamped to teenage bedrooms as adults feared for the introspection and 'addiction' that allegedly resulted; the Internet's chat rooms, formerly the haunts of the geeky and gauche, are now the playground of the school student; the upwardly mobile executive's finest status symbol the mobile phone is now invading the classroom (and children actually use the messaging that the executives never understood!). Throughout all this, predictably enough, parents and teachers worried loudly and publicly about pop music induced deafness, computer games addiction, safety (and costs) on the Internet and microwave radiation.

Health risks may or may not be real but the difficulty with this deficiency model of children – as passive or naive victims of the ebbs and flows of technological life – is that it blinds us to the quality and complexity of the strategies that children evolve to use, and subvert, new technologies to their social, entertainment and learning lives. Because we see each new activity as 'a problem' we miss the opportunity either to harness children's emerging capabilities or to offer a progression and continuity to them. Nowhere is this such a clear waste of both potential and opportunity as in children's new literacy, the subject of this foreword.

Literacy is, of course, always a product of some technology in the very real sense that whatever transmission and representational form we adopt as a vehicle for our narratives will depend entirely on the technology of the moment, from prehistoric cave painting, through Babylonian cuniform to algebra or the notation of modern dance. Notational technology – with all its inadequacies – has arguably served us well as a recording technology, although there are many – Sir Paul McCartney, for example – who would argue that any form of notation would, or has, imposed itself on their creativity.

The ability to read and digest, then re-present and display in some notational form has long been a functional definition of a literate person. Interestingly, the ability to storytell, to speak in public, to show and tell has also been historically valued as a mark of a literate citizen. In both reading and writing though the citizen is a prisoner of the technology of the age and this can be wildly distorting. The move from storytelling to the printed narrative of *Beowulf* produced a well-documented change in the power relationship of information providers but back in the twentieth century the inability of recording technology to offer better than the notational representation of writing was responsible for the collapse of oracy in the UK curriculum. Everyone – teachers, employers, students, parents – was agreed that oracy mattered but a national education ethos that distrusted teachers' judgement wanted that judgement moderated and moderating the spoken word and measuring spoken contributions with any eye to quality of consistency was just too complex; the technology of the moment failed us so we dropped oracy and in doing so, of course, failed the children too. Pens were always technology with all its limits and opportunity, just as computers are today, once again allowing oracy to be valued for example. However, as the technology of literacy broadens and progresses it stops getting in the way of what we want to do, substituting the question: 'What exactly can I do?' with the far tougher question: 'You can do anything you like, so what would you like to do?'

All too often the unimaginative answer is simply to do whatever we did before a little better or faster and hope to represent this as progress, which it isn't. Computers are great productivity tools for producing textual communication – as the reams of paper spewing out of every office printer in the world will confirm – but they are also tools for new forms of creative storytelling as an increasingly democratized publishing industry from desktop publishing through fanzines to websites and beyond will also confirm. For now, computers remain relatively expensive and we have to make tough choices about the way that we harness them in our creative learning lives – do we simply use them to do the old tasks faster or use them to engage children in the new digital creativity, and literacy, that we see all around us?

There is very little debate to be had; even the workaday example of children writing with a plain word processor is not the use of a productivity tool to write faster or with fewer errors. Those children are using a tool that fundamentally changes the processes that they are engaged in, with new strategies for editing and authoring, new help from spelling, grammar and summary tools, new awarenesses of the semiotics of typeface and layout. The old task is dead, long live the new task! The problem comes when we try to set old tasks for new process and report of this as progress. For example, we have all too often heard the howl of staff-room anguish that 'they just cut stuff from a CD-encyclopaedia and pasted it into their work without thinking'. Once again, a deficiency model of children masks the real issue; this cry reflects not on the foolishness of children or the inadequacies of computers but on a failure of the classroom or homework task set to acknowledge the new processes and tools available. With these new tools more stretching and creative tasks need to be set and better assessment strategies devised. Paradoxically some try to represent a word-processed 'slightly better essay' as progress, by comparing it uncritically to a handwritten one ('Look, it's longer and with fewer mistakes') but, in practice, the old task should be wildly exceeded given the quality of support tools the young writer has at their disposal. How much better should children perform the old task with new tools? Ten per cent better? Twenty per cent better? Five times better? In practice it doesn't matter because the new processes that our learners are engaged in supplant the old products; the processes of writing become more important for the developing critical awareness of a young author than the resultant products. We see a new literacy emerging which stretches beyond the technologically imposed limits (the inadequate old pen, remember?) of our previous tasks.

The good, but challenging, news is that where technology once let us down by failing to support oracy it now supports such a wide portfolio of possibilities and processes that we face some challenging new choices (or, put less tactfully, some huge problems). Using a computer children can represent their creativity with text, graphics, speech, video, animation and more, they can do it at school or away from school, singly and in private or collaboratively and en masse, synchronously or spread across a long time period. But which subsets of those choices would we regard as necessary for base literacy? It is not hard to look around the world and find examples of gifted storytellers and communicators who struggled to write in a linear hand. Should we continue to regard them as illiterate or embrace in the portfolio of literacy the new media that technology offers us? And at what age might we give up on one strand of that portfolio – writing or speech perhaps – to concentrate on reinforcing and progressing the others? Looking around the world in an attempt to elicit standards does not help and may well hinder. In 1996 the Japanese group Keizai Doyukai – similar in role to the UK's Confederation of British Industry – took a long and searching look at the Japanese education system and its under-performing economy. Where was the source of the inspiration that had produced the Walkman and that made a step change in motorcycle design? Considerable effort was expended in testing Japanese school students and in comparing their scores to those of their peers around the world. Japanese education could be honourably presented as 'world class', but something important was missing; they concluded that:

> The post-war education system in Japan sought to eliminate deviations in students and deliver an equal, uniform education throughout the land. This was effective in reaching the goal of catching up industrialised nations. Now however, the nation is in need of highly creative and independent individuals. Fostering individuals with these characteristics will require educational reform starting from the elementary level and taking at least 10–20 years to be effective.

Japan being Japan, a start was made right there and then, embracing ICT to help develop, but not provide, that creativity.

Of all the capabilities that our school students develop, creativity is probably the one most likely to vouchsafe our economic growth and our ranking position in the league table of world economies. Of the many things that children do at school or at home the one least likely to be replaced by a computer's capability is creativity. For that reason it is no surprise that around the world the children of those who are working right at the cutting edge of ICT are subtly encouraged by their 'wired' parents into music, drama and art. But these families still have rooms cluttered with computers; creativity is not the antithesis of the computer, far from it.

Encouragingly, much of the pioneering work with ICT in the UK has stressed the computer's creative uses. Trawling through the dusty assets of the UK's National Archive of Educational Computing it is quickly apparent that the ability to make or create with a computer – whether it was images, music, software or text – was what caught our attention in those first primitive days of tape loading programs and incomprehensible code. Interestingly enough, those early computers and the creative children who harnessed them provided the foundations of our phenomenally successful computer software industry, a link still appreciated by the current government. According to Chris Smith MP, Secretary of State for Culture, Media and Sport, 'Creativity in its widest sense is at the heart of what we in this country are good at. It is the foundation of a new generation of high-tech, high-skill industries.'

But children working creatively with a computer require us to accept a diversity and uncertainty of outcomes as they exceed even our most ambitious expectations for their progress. If we are to move forward, we need to accept that standards do not require standardization and inspection teams need to be helped to value creativity above conformity and content. Base capabilities still matter, they are of course a basic right, but in 1999 government think tank Demos confirmed that: 'Creative application of knowledge cannot be practised within a predefined curriculum structure if it is focussed too heavily on content, at the expense of depth of understanding and breadth of application.'

We must strive to ensure that computers are harnessed to that creativity, understanding and breadth of application. We need a national push to put great creative software tools onto our children's screens and to exclude the testing tools until computers are no longer scarce. Walking around many school computer facilities it is depressing how often they feature notices about what must not be done. Creative ICT schools celebrate the unexpected and reveal how it was done; it is a lesson the UK examination and curriculum structures have yet to learn. Our economic future depends on them learning it.

PROFESSOR STEPHEN HEPPELL

Introduction

New Literacies, New Technologies?

Nikki Gamble

When I was preparing this introduction I was given a review copy of a children's picture book, *The Cultivated Wolf*, illustrated by Pascal Biet, story by Becky Bloom (1999). As I read the book I found that the issues I was writing about were embedded in this children's story. And so I will start with some storytelling. The story begins:

> After many days' walking, the hungry Wolf . . . wandered into a quiet little town. He was tired and hungry and his feet were aching and he had only a little money that he kept for emergencies. Then he remembered. There's a farm outside this village, he thought. I'll find some food there . . .

The skinny, naked, ravening wolf behaves in the manner readers of traditional stories have come to expect; by attacking the farm and threatening to eat the animals. But the animals' reaction is not predictable; they do not run and hide in their houses. Although the illiterate chickens and rabbits run for their lives, the cow, the pig and the duck are too engrossed in the books they are reading to care about the wolf. 'Just ignore it,' says the duck. 'This is a farm for cultivated animals,' says the pig. Like a young child there is nothing the wolf dislikes more than being ignored and he determines to learn to read and write so that he too may become 'a cultivated animal'. And indeed he does go to school and learns to read. He returns to the farm, now sporting a pair of spectacles (the human trappings are significant), and begins to read:

> Run, Wolf! Run!
> See Wolf run.

But this 'barking at print', familiar to teachers and young readers whose early reading experiences included Key Words Reading Scheme, Peter and Jane books, isn't good enough for the cultivated animals; they simply aren't impressed.

The Wolf jumped back over the fence and ran . . . straight to the public library. (The natural story language provides a delightful contrast with the book the wolf has been reading.)

This time he returns to the farm armed with a story book, having now acquired a waistcoat to go with his spectacles. He reads:

OnceuponatimetherewerethreelittlepigsOnedaytheirmothercalledthemand toldthem . . .

But, of course, this is no good either. Finally the wolf goes to the bookshop and buys his very first book. Returning to the farm (now wearing a hat):

He lay down on the grass, made himself comfortable, took out his new book and began to read.

In the final double page spread pig hands the wolf an apple like Eve welcoming Adam to the world of knowledge. But there is no shame in this Eden. The wolf has taken responsibility for his own learning, achieving a state of independence and autonomy. The wolf proves that under his wolfskin he possesses essentially human qualities; 'a human in wolf's clothing'. He is a confident and passionate storyteller and his new friends are enthralled with his talent. The story ends with the promise of eternal summer afternoons and the sharing of endless tales. And one notices in the detail of the illustration 'the cultivated animals' sharing their experiences with the rabbits who are also beginning to show an interest in books.

This fable contains a positive and profound message for young readers about the power of books, and especially *stories*, to transform, heal and educate. In this tale literacy, as Grace Kempster reminds us in Chapter 3, is regarded as 'a means not an end in itself'.

In reading *The Cultivated Wolf* I am reminded of Barbara Hardy's seminal work 'Narrative as a Primary Act of Mind' (1968) in Margaret Meek *et al.* (1977). She writes:

narrative . . . is not to be regarded as an aesthetic invention used by artists to control, manipulate, and order experience, but as a primary act of mind transferred from life to art. (p.12)

Hardy goes on to describe how narrative pervades everyday experiences:

What concerns me here are the qualities which fictional narrative shares that inner and outer storytelling that plays a major role in our sleeping and waking lives. For we dream in narrative, daydream in narrative, remember, anticipate, hope, despair, believe, doubt, plan, revise, criticize, construct, gossip, learn, hate and love by narrative. (p.13)

In *The Cultivated Wolf* imaginative stories have become part of the wolf's way of life, he is a fully integrated 'person'. The endpapers provide the contrast showing the pre-literate and post-literate wolf. At the beginning of the book we are presented with a bleak picture, characters seem to act in isolation and the wolf is treated with suspicion. At the end of the book, however, the wolf is surrounded by new friends and the local children gather round to hear his stories and the remaining characters are facing him. But wolf's life is also presented as a story with a clear enticing moment, development of conflict, climax, resolution and coda. The stories we tell about ourselves and to ourselves are the essence of life.

So how does this traditional, romantic and idealized image of the reading experience relate to literacy and the new technologies? In this technological age some commentators have lamented what they see as the inevitable negative implications of children spending more time playing with their computer and video games. For example, Sven Birkerts (1995) perceives a threat to verbal articulation and mental passion that are nurtured through sustained reading. His concern emphasizes children's inability to concentrate, and particularly to focus, on the written word or to engage in a more reflective approach to text. He goes on to ask, 'If a person turns from print finding it too slow, too hard, irrelevant to the excitement of the present, then what happens to that person's sense of culture and continuity?' Though there are legitimate concerns about the low-level content quality and possible addictive effects of the shoot 'em up and platform games, which should not too readily be dismissed by ardent advocates of the new technologies, it is also important to engage in balanced appraisal to research the actual, rather than the feared, impact of these technologies.

My personal experience suggests that computer games and an interest in reading books are not antithetical. I am an enthusiastic games player but the appeal of exciting, challenging games hasn't dulled my appetite for reading; it isn't a case of computers *or* books. I read and use an eclectic range of texts for different purposes, at different times, to meet different needs. When using CD-ROM games I am drawn into the narrative in similar ways to when I read Dickens or Atwood, enjoy 30 seconds of the new instalment in the Nescafé Saga, share an apocryphal story with friends after dinner or catch up with the lives of the characters in a docusoap.

And children also have the capacity to develop their personal narratives from a wide range of texts. Carol Fox's (1993) research clearly demonstrates links between children's imaginative play and narrative fiction:

> let children retell, act out and write down these stories too. However 'unsuitable' or predictable some of us might think they are . . . [they] are hardly anodyne and compare well to fairy tales in terms of their powerful themes. (p. 194)

The cross-fertilization works across different media. As I write my seven-year-old son and his friend have just finished a session on the Playstation and are involved in making a game in which their favourite Pokémon, Ekans, is waging battle against Lord Voldemort in his quest to keep Voldemort from stealing the Philosopher's Stone. They are painstakingly involved with making maps and diagrams that look remarkably like the screens from the Pokémon Gameboy version. (This is a child who can take half an hour to write two words in a literacy lesson.) A case of Nintendo meets *Harry Potter*! Occasionally I hear announcements like 'End of Part One'. Their game is a composite drawn from different sources using archetypal themes and characters and structural elements of television with a narrative thread binding the mix together. If there is a problem here, it is one of the value we attach to the narratives children select and enjoy which need to be acknowledged within the educational context.

When I talk to students preparing for teaching practice about their planned use of ICT to support reading it is often the talking book that they refer to in the first instance. Talking books are the most obvious connection to a traditional literacy model using conventions associated with reading books such as turning pages and a narrator's voice. Motivating though these materials might be with their interactive hotspots they do not, on the whole, exploit the potential of the new technologies in a way that advances the definition of literacy. Rather they depend on what Stephen Heppell refers to in the Foreword as setting old tasks for new processes and representing them as progress. In Chapter 1 Sue Brindley addresses the conceptual leap from thinking about ICT as a support for traditional literacy to flexible definitions which take account of human interaction with technology.

However, to be literate is more than being able to read and write at a functional level. It is about access to ideas that challenge our thinking and promote new ways of looking at our world. Margaret Meek, *How Texts Teach What Readers Learn* (1988), demonstrates that *what* children read is vitally important. Structures of texts determine what readers are able to learn and some texts provide more challenge than others. The post-modern picture book has many examples of texts produced in innovative ways that encourage readers to stop and look again. In these examples illustration is not used to decorate the page or simply provide visual description for the written text; the full meaning of the book lies in neither the text nor the pictures but in the 'gap' that lies between them.

Gaps are an important concept in challenging texts which encourage readers to make their own closures. Here Iser (1974) explains the theory drawn from Gestalt psychology:

These gaps have a different effect on the process of anticipation and retrospection, and thus on the 'gestalt' of the virtual dimension, for they may be filled in different ways. For this reason, one text is potentially capable of several different realizations, and no reading can ever exhaust the full potential, for each individual reader will fill in the gaps in his own way, thereby excluding the various other possibilities; as he reads he will make his own decision as to how the gap is to be filled. In this very act the dynamics of reading are revealed . . . With traditional texts this process was more or less unconscious, but modern texts frequently exploit it deliberately. (p. 280)

Multimedia texts also have this potential. I freely admit that my most exciting computer based 'reading' experiences have come from playing games, not programs specifically designed for educational purposes or the edutainment market where the didactic element is often emphasized at the expense of creative possibilities. Of course this problem exists with books too; when curriculum relevance rather than creative desire leads the development of new material, the result is rarely great literature.

Currently it is the games market which seems to make most innovative use of hypertext's non-linear format. One of the most interesting and compelling games is Cyan's (1993) award-winning *Myst* and its sequel *Riven* (1997). *Myst* is an adventure game set on the island which has been created by a wizard/scientist/anthropologist, Atrus, who is imprisoned in another dimension. The island of Myst is disintegrating and the player must halt this process and rescue Atrus. This is achieved by solving logic puzzles and assembling clues that are picked up through close observation to aural and visual detail. Hyperlinks connect from Myst to other ages or dimensions which the player must visit before completing the final task. The chronology of the narrative will be different for each player, although ultimately the choices are restricted as particular tasks serve to set up the conditions for the end game.

Myst is particularly interesting because it is essentially a non-populated game; the island appears to be uninhabited so that the player (or players if this is a collaborative experience as it often is) becomes the main protagonist; unlike other games where this role is projected onto a character which the player controls. This affects the focalization of the narrative, drawing the player into the story through the use of similar techniques to those employed in virtual reality. It is evident that the player is, to use Iser's words, 'creating instead of merely observing'. Play can take place without any on-screen icons to act as a barrier to the beautifully realized settings which creates a feeling of immediacy as though the story is set in present time unlike most narrative fiction which is set in the past. The player must work out how to proceed by learning from experience. At first the game may seem very slow as there is plenty of space and time for reflection and no action. Information is slowly accumulated and the significance of an object or letter may only come to light after many hours of play. The player may experience uncertainty and anticipation as though this 'story' is happening to them. *Myst* is an example of a multimedia text that requires a different kind of reading. It is a text with gaps that 'show' rather than 'tell' us the narrative, though it uses different structures and devices to modernist fiction or the picture book. It is a pity that there is a tendency to overexplain and narrow down interpretation as the game draws to a close. It would be good to see producers writing more genuinely open-ended games in the future. Furthermore, although there are many adventure fantasy games there are not many that have the same qualities as *Myst*. And I have not yet seen any that are written for a target child audience.

Novelty is not enough to make a program challenging and satisfying. Programs must be well written not just by programers but in collaboration with good authors. In Chapter 6 Becky James looks closely at three multimedia texts and considers the potential readings they elicit. Hypertext also offers fresh possibilities for young authors to think divergently about text and very young children can produce this kind of text. A framework for looking at the literacy opportunity afforded by the use of hypertext is proposed by Richard Millwood in Chapter 4.

Returning to *The Cultivated Wolf* we notice that the wolf is motivated by a desire to be included; to belong to a community of readers. Similarly, in observing children at the computer, what is immediately apparent is the social discourse and confidence with which they are able to talk about technology. The phenomenon of solitary child playing in their own room is not as widespread as might be feared and is probably indicative of factors other than, or additional to, the seductive, hypnotic allure of the computer. Children, I have found, want to share their computer experiences. New technology provides an opportunity to create a global literacy club where children communicate with each other via Internet web pages, chat sites and e-mail. It is conceivable that the PC can be used as a democratic tool to share information where books and ideas are censored or forbidden. Access to a PC can offer a degree of inclusiveness to isolated individuals who are hospitalized, home bound or living in remote areas. This potential is explored in Chapter 5 where Nick Easingwood evaluates the use of electronic mail in the classroom. And in some instances technological support can act as an equalizer for children who experience difficulties with reading. Angela McGlashon takes this further in Chapter 9 which outlines some specific ways in which computer technology can facilitate literacy and learning for pupils with special educational needs.

In its simple moral conclusion *The Cultivated Wolf* suggests that the achievement of literacy is unequivocally good but, of course, there is nothing inherently good about literacy or technology; it is the uses we make of it that count. New literacies like the traditional ones can be used for positive or negative ends. Questions have been raised about the moral issues concerning genuine accessibility and inclusiveness and the possibility that some sections of society will be disadvantaged in the technological society. There are also issues to do with regulation and easy accessibility of illegal material which may be inadvertently downloaded from the Internet. Recently my son asked if we could search for some information about the Spice Girls on the Internet. We found over 300 items but none of them related to the pop group! Furthermore, before making claims about the democratic potential offered by the personal computer we should pause to give some consideration to the economics of production.

A literate person makes judgements about the quality and value of information. The Internet presents new challenges in the way items are presented, where equal weight can be given to the treatment of a worldwide catastrophe and the Pamela Anderson website. Whether the Internet is used destructively or creatively is determined by the user's ability to make judgements and literacy is the prerequisite.

As has been suggested the Internet offers flexibility in both mode and place of learning. It is perhaps an intended irony that the cultivated wolf was least successful in the school environment. In Chapter 3 Grace Kempster describes ways in which the public library service is incorporating networked systems that extend their capacity to provide educative support, and in Chapter 7 Sarah Mears evaluates the potential of websites that are created for young readers and the role of reader services in helping to develop the autonomous learner. Libraries are exciting places and unlike the highly regulated environment of school, there is more scope to offer young learners freedom to choose. The learning that is self-directed and managed is the most powerful. And in the twenty-first century we may well see more varied and imaginative education provision.

There are professional implications for teachers and teacher trainers who must work within the current structures but in ways that are flexible enough to accommodate rapid growth and change. The terms literacy and technology are often used in rhetoric associated with preparing a workforce but curriculum that emphasizes key skills at the expense of knowledge and creativity is unlikely to meet those needs. *ICT and Literacy* concludes with a consideration of these implications for the individual teacher. In Chapter 8 Marilyn Foreman, and, more broadly for training and course design in Chapter 10, Nick Easingwood and Nikki Gamble, discuss key considerations not only for the present but also for the future.

The main issue facing those of us who work in education is, I think, perfectly encapsulated by John Abbott, quoted in DfEE *All Our Futures* (1999a)

> Life is more than work. If we give children the idea that they need high-level skills only for work, we have got it all wrong. They are going to need even higher level skills to perform in a democratic society. We have got to get this absolutely right: the issue is not technology (and I would add literacy) but what it means to be human, what kind of future we want for the human race. (p. 23)

REFERENCES

Printed texts

Biet, P. and Bloom, B. (1999) *The Cultivated Wolf*, London: Siphano Picture Books.
Birkerts, S. (1995) *The Gutenberg Elegies: The Fate of Reading in an Electronic Age*, New York: Fawcett Columbine.

DfEE (1999a) *All Our Futures: Creativity, Culture and Education*, London: HMSO.
DfEE (1999b) *The National Curriculum for England*, London: HMSO.
Fox, C. (1993) *At the Very Edge of the Forest: The Influence of Literature on Storytelling by Children*, London: Cassell.
Iser, W. (1974) *The Implied Reader*, Baltimore, MD: Johns Hopkins University Press.
Meek, M., Warlow, A. and Barton, G. (1977) *The Cool Web*, London: Bodley Head.
Meek, M. (1998) *How Texts Teach What Readers Learn*, Thimble Press.
Murray, W. (1964) *Peter and Jane*, Key Words Reading Scheme, Loughborough: Ladybird Books.
Papert, S. (1993) *The Children's Machine: Rethinking School in the Age of the Computer*, New York: Basic Books.

Multimedia

Cyan Productions (1993) *Myst*, Cleveland: Red Orb Entertainment, Broderbund.
Cyan Productions (1997) *Riven*, Cleveland: Red Orb Entertainment, Broderbund.

Part One
THEORETICAL PERSPECTIVES

Chapter 1

ICT and Literacy

Sue Brindley

INTRODUCTION

ICT (Information and Communications Technology) stands in interesting relation to literacy, being as it is capable both of supporting and promoting the basic skills of reading and writing – the dominant classroom definition of literacy (Papert, 1993). Yet it carries with it the inevitability of extending that definition into a model of literacy which acknowledges, *sine qua non*, that literacy is a dynamic concept extending beyond the basic acquisition of reading and writing skills. It also opens up a further dimension of literacy – that the basic skills model is a limited interpretation of literacy and that the acquisition and development of literacy skills responds to a new taxonomy almost in direct response to the linking of ICT with literacy.

This chapter is therefore divided into three sections: literacy as a basic skill and the use of ICT in promoting that area; the role of ICT in redefining literacy to meet the needs of a post-print society; and a proposed new taxonomy of literacy skills which restructure thinking on ICT and literacy.

WHO DEFINES LITERACY?

Literacy in the classroom – what Margaret Meek refers to as 'schooled' literacy (1991, p. 124) – has been given a high profile in the British government's National Literacy Strategy (DfEE, 1998a). Prior to this, schooled literacy focused mainly on reading (Meek, 1991, p. 30) with the debate about teaching reading, stylized as the phonics/real books debate, dominating both public and professional concerns. Reading as the major focus of literacy emerged again when the Secretary of State for Education, David Blunkett, in establishing the Literacy Task Force, stated that 'By the end of a second term of Labour government, all children leaving primary school will have reached a reading age of at least eleven' (DfEE, 1998). The establishment of the National Year of

Reading, one of the 'key strands in the Government's National Literacy Strategy' (DfEE, 1998a) echoes this preoccupation. Writing, with the notable exception of the work of Graves (1983) on conferencing, had trailed behind in the high stakes debate, unless used for a vehicle of despair about the standards of spelling, grammar or handwriting.

Nevertheless, documentation produced at government policy level, and in particular the *Framework for Teaching* (DfEE, 1998a), has a balanced perspective with an 'official' definition of literacy emerging via the work of the National Literacy Project. This includes writing, along with an acknowledgement of the role of speaking and listening, in developing literacy skills. It states that:

> Literacy unites the important skills of reading and writing. It also involves speaking and listening, which, although they are not identified separately in the Framework, are an essential part of it. Good oral work enhances pupils' understanding of language in both oral and written forms . . . It is also an important part of the process through which pupils read and compose texts. (*Op. cit.*, p.3)

Literacy is defined in this context by the National Curriculum standing orders for English, although literacy should be actively taught across all subjects. ICT receives no specific reference in the Framework, although the document entitled *Implementation of the National Literacy Strategy* (DfEE, 1997b) includes a recommendation that for secondary schools OFSTED should record, among other data, 'the contribution of information and communication technology to literacy teaching . . .'.

It becomes clear that in classroom literacy, as constructed by policy documents, ICT is virtually invisible and no separate literacy requirement is recognized in relation to, for example, reading screen-based texts. Literacy is rooted firmly in an understanding of word level (phonics, spelling and vocabulary), sentence level (grammar and punctuation) and text level (comprehension and composition), traditional approaches to the teaching of reading and writing in the primary school. The contribution of ICT in developing schooled literacy is potentially immense. However, the highly prescriptive approach of the Literacy Hour with the emphasis on whole-class teaching and shared reading offers no encouragement to develop the use of ICT. Perhaps equally powerfully, ICT does not figure at all in the mechanism to be used for ascertaining success in developing literacy skills, Key Stage 2 SATs in English. There is little encouragement for teachers who are not confident in their use of ICT to become pedagogically adventurous in their approach to schooled literacy. Despite research evidence that ICT can enhance the development of reading, writing, and speaking and listening skills (see, for example: Balestri, 1988; Hunter, 1988; Papert, 1993; Woolley, 1993; Scrimshaw, 1993 and Loveless, 1995) and the production of materials to support such development (see, for example, *Information Technology in the Primary and National Curriculum*, Hampshire LEA, 1995; *IT in English*, DfEE, 1997a). Without training and support for teachers, the use of ICT adds little to literacy development (Eraut and Hoyles, 1989; Snyder, 1994b). The brief of the literacy consultants employed by Local Education Authorities in England and Wales does not currently extend to exploiting ICT in the development of literacy skills. Anecdotal evidence on local training for the Literacy Hour reveals that some authorities are encouraging the use of ICT, while others make no mention of it.

REDEFINING LITERACY

It is my contention that schooled literacy, which traditionally sees the acquisition of the ability to construct and interpret text as largely an individual activity, bounded by the concept of text as linear and fixed, is no longer adequate. That the term 'computer literate' part of current teaching discourse is in itself indicative that the notion of literacy has shifted in schools. There is an ongoing tension for schools between the professional understandings of the ways in which the curriculum should be responsive to a changing society and the demands placed on schools by the statutory requirements of the National Curriculum and associated assessment arrangements. Ironically, it is the ICT initial teacher training requirements for England and Wales (Annex B, Government *Circular 4/98*, DfEE, 1998a) with the clear emphasis on subject delivery that is likely to bring about the shift in understanding of literacy so long overdue.

In schools, being a computer-literate student has largely meant acquiring a technical expertise that enables a competent use of the available hardware. However, a much more complex and exciting understanding of computer literacy is available and it is a lifelong literacy. This entails the ability to construct and manipulate text, which is not seen as linear but multidimensional and multimedia and which is no longer fixed but infinitely changeable. The model here is far closer to that required by school leavers at the beginning of the new millennium's world of literacy where, for example, writing is rarely undertaken as an individual task and text too is constantly subjected to changes and revisions not simply as a matter of style but in order to accommodate the rapid shifts in information being made available. Similarly, such information may well be accessed using the Internet, when reading skills need to extend beyond book print to screen print, with the inclusion of graphics and an understanding of page layout and hyperlinks. Literacy here means knowing that effective information acquisition requires an understanding of how texts are constructed; otherwise readers become trapped in a model of reading which requires them to read screens sequentially simply in order to gain one piece of information buried somewhere in the text. The argument here is that a truly 'computer-literate' student would be able to access this information with greater speed and accuracy by virtue of understanding the construction of text on screen and of the text search facilities available to them.

In *The Children's Machine* (1993), Papert offers one such definition of literacy. His view is that 'becoming literate means thinking differently than one did previously, seeing the world differently' (p. 10). Papert's contention is that 'traditional' – schooled – literacy is better described as letteracy. Letteracy in Papert's terms can be achieved independently of the acquisition of literacy. Literacy is the broader canvas. ICT is the medium of access and construction. In many ways, however, letteracy and literacy can go together. Many teachers already use ICT imaginatively to consolidate schooled literacy. In the case of reading Adam and Wild (1997) describe the use of CD-ROM interactive storybooks and report that 'students can interact with the character and landscape, to hear sounds and speech, and see animation. This type of interaction is not possible with books or print media' (Anderson, 1992).

They go on to discuss the control the reader has over the text, including choices on who reads (the reader, the screen narrator or both together). The reader enters, they contend, a world of 'other levels of language and learning'. Interactive books also carry research evidence of the extension of vocabulary (Elley, 1989) and supporting students in both phonic development and early recognition of word families (Freebody, 1992). Further research evidence (Ring *et al.*, 1994) indicates that 90 per cent of a sample group of students preferred the CD-ROM version of the story compared to the traditional printed version. These findings are supported by Miller *et al.* (1994) who also conclude that there are 'positive reading outcomes using the technology', a position also held by Grabe and Dossman (1988). Motivation is clearly a significant factor here and the work of Lancy and Hayes (1988) particularly demonstrates that reluctant readers spent significantly more time reading interactive books than print books.

ICT supporting the teaching and learning of writing carries with it a similar range of evidence. There has been evidence that teachers initially used ICT to correct secretarial features. Snyder (1994a) reports in her study of six classrooms that

> Each of the teachers emphasised the importance of correctness in writing and the publishing capabilities of the technology so that it was used primarily for transcription and printing of a 'good copy' . . . None explored how the technology could be used effectively as an integral part of computer mediated writing pedagogy. The focus in all six classrooms was on operationalising the technology, not on exploring its capacities to develop students' writing. (p. 62)

This may go some way to explaining the findings of Roblyer *et al.* (1988) and Montague (1990) who reported mixed results on studies of writing quality, with some evidence that revisions to work were superficial rather than substantial.

There is increasing evidence, however, that ICT is being used increasingly to support and develop writing practice in schools beyond the superficial. Adams and Brindley (1998) report on a school in Canada which is conducting a pilot study of a class of 16-year-olds, working entirely on an ICT-based curriculum constructed around an industry-based model of projects and tasks. The work was undertaken in connection with communities beyond the classroom, including authors providing feedback to students on their fiction writing. Writing was found to be purposeful and a keen awareness of audience needs was recognized through the production of accurately spelt and grammatically correct text. Writing was often undertaken collaboratively and good oracy skills were an integral part of the writing process, as clearly outlined in the influential work of Graves (1983) on developing a community of writers. That letteracy and literacy can develop together is perhaps illustrated by one event in the classroom. During the research, one pupil, who had been functionally illiterate on his entry to class and who, now one year on, was first encountered sitting in front of a computer reading (the book) *Anne of Green Gables*, said that he 'wanted to know what everyone else was doing on the computers, so he had better learn to read so as to find out what was on that little screen that got everyone else so fired up'.

Clearly the type of writing tasks undertaken extended beyond the traditional story or report writing and the use of e-mail to communicate beyond the classroom was extensive. This new writing skill brings about a different literacy capacity (see, for example, Abbott, 1996; Perkins and Newman, 1995). The contention here is that e-mail sits somewhere between writing and oracy but follows the rules of neither. However, research undertaken by Littleton *et al.* (1998) indicates that students can

> spend far longer over composing an e-mail, paying far more attention to details, spelling and conveying meaning than in traditional classroom writing because the audience they are writing for is authentic. There is a real purpose in their writing in that they are attempting to communicate with children in other classrooms or other schools.

Even in this small sample of reading and writing activities, it is impossible not to acknowledge the impact ICT has had on the development of literacy skills, in terms of both purpose and realization. The broader definition has emerged, *inter alia*, and almost without formal recognition from the policy-makers.

Papert (1993) describes the emerging model as making progress towards a new form of literacy that encompasses a range of media by which students learn and by which they communicate. This new form of literacy can take the form of learning through a range of media (Loveless, 1995) in which the ability to read, speak and write is complemented, enhanced and sometimes replaced by photographic and video images, graphics and sound. Students can convey meaning in the most appropriate form for the task in hand using the tools they feel best equipped to use.

LITERACY ACQUISITION

If the broader definition of literacy is acknowledged – that is that ICT reinvents the text – a further area of development opens up for literacy. Schooled literacy was taught in order to access texts. Most students expected to leave primary school as literate and for those who did not, secondary schools provided learning support until they were literate or until they left school to become adult illiterates. Literacy was a basic skill, a one-off hurdle to be cleared and then pretty much forgotten. The new literacy, however, cannot be contained in the same way. There clearly exists a need to reconsider literacy as an ongoing development – referred to earlier as lifelong literacy. The acquisition of the new literacy cannot be ticked off at eleven. Instead, while acknowledging the need for basic schooled literacy, there should be a further taxonomy of literacy skills acknowledged: basic, extended and advanced literacy skills, reflecting changes made in reading and writing demands through ICT. Extended literacy, for example, would include the understanding of text beyond the linear and the differing demands made on the reader encountering this type of text. It would need to include information literacy as defined by the National Grid for Learning which states that

> a definition of network literacy [is] the capacity to use electronic networks to access resources, to create resources, and to communicate with others. These estimates of network literacy can be seen as extensions of the traditional skills of reading (and) writing . . . This is of central importance and provide(s) a link with the Government's focus on improving standards of literacy . . . (p. 10)

Advanced literacy would demonstrate the sophisticated understanding of the construction of text with a spatial dimension, the interaction of text with graphics, which in turn may require interaction from the reader, who may then become the writer. In one sense, it is a post-structuralist view of text. But this does not alter the concept out of existence – quite the opposite in that such texts already exist with, for example, Richard Lanham's *The Electronic Word* (1995). In schools, advanced literacy skills are already evident in the use of hypertext. Birkets (1994) explores the use of hypertext in collaborative writing, 'trading lines, writing parallel texts that merge, moving independently created sets of characters in and out of communal fiction space'. He cites Coover's work (1992) in which he and a group of students established a hypertext hotel,

> A place where writers were free to check in, to open new rooms, new corridors, new intrigues, to unlink texts to create new links, to intrude on or sabotage the texts of others, to alter plot trajectories, then kill off one another's characters or even sabotage the hotel's plumbing. (p. 160)

In much the same way as literary theory was seen as a challenge to the very definition of literature and literary analysis, hypertext is seen as a challenge to canonical and established text and thereby traditional literacy skills. But hypertext exists and cannot be un-invented; indeed, a new technical language is emerging in relation to it. And as with literary theory, not too much time will pass before hypertext itself becomes part of the established way of reading and writing. The question is: will schools be enabled to teach the advanced skills required or will dogged adherence to schooled literacy place UK students at an educational and economic disadvantage compared with students outside the UK? Consider, for example, the statement made by Professor Douglas Young of the University of Cape Town, South Africa which has been incorporated into the South African government's policy statement on language:

> literacy has expanded to include several types of literacies. 'Literacies' stresses the issue of access to the world and to knowledge through development of multiple capacities within all of us to make sense of our worlds through whatever means we have, not only texts and books.

The move to a post-print world brought about by ICT and the new definitions of literacy emerging should be seen as a welcome event   an acknowledgement that society and, therefore, education are dynamic. Redefining literacy is one part of the recognition we have that learning to 'access the world . . . and knowledge' is critical to our present and future society.

Some say there is a literacy crisis, but this is just our modern way of drawing attention to what we think is important. (Meek, 1991, p. 9)

REFERENCES

Abbott, C. (1996) 'Young people developing a new language: the implications for teachers and for education of electronic discourse', paper presented at informal seminar, Institute for Educational Technology, Open University.

Adam, N. and Wild, M. (1997) 'Applying CD-ROM interactive storybooks to learning to read', *Journal of Computer Assisted Learning*, **13**: 119–32.

Adams, A. and Brindley, S. (1998) 'Computers and collaborative writing', *Journal of IT in Teacher Education*.

Anderson, J. (1992) 'Living books and other books without pages', *Unicorn*, **18**(3).

Balestri, D. P. (1988) 'Softcopy and hard: word processing and writing process', *Academic Computing* February:14–17; 41–5.

Birkerts, S. (1994) *The Gutenberg Elegies: The Fate of Reading in an Electronic Age*, New York: Fawcett Columbine.

Coover, R. (1992) 'The end of books', *New York Times Book Review*, 21 June.

DfEE (1997a) *IT in English*, Coventry: National Council for Educational Technology.

DfEE (1997b) *The Implementation of the Literacy Strategy*, London: HMSO.

DfEE (1997c) *Connecting the Learning Society*, London: DfEE.

DfEE (1998a) *The National Literacy Strategy: Framework for Teaching*, London: HMSO.

DfEE (1998b) *National Year of Reading*, London: HMSO.

DfEE (1998c) *Teaching: High Status, High Standards*, London: DfEE.

Elley, W. (1989) 'Vocabulary acquisition from listening to stories', *Reading Research Quarterly*, **24**: 174–87.

Eraut, M. and Hoyles, C. (1989) 'Group work with computers', *Journal of Computer Assisted Learning*, 5: 12–24.

Freebody, P. (1992) 'A socio-cultural approach: Resourcing four roles as a literacy learner', in A. Watson and A. Badenhop (eds) *Prevention of Reading Failure*, Sydney: Ashton.

Grabe, M. and Dossman, M. (1988) 'The potential of adventure games for the development of reading and study skills', *Journal of Computer Based Instruction*, **15**(2): 72–7.

Graves, D. (1983) *Writing: Children and Teachers at Work*, London: Heinemann.

Hampshire LEA (1995) *Information Technology in the Primary Curriculum*.

Hunter, P. (1988) 'The writing process and word processing', *Microscope Special: Writing*, 3–8.

Kimberley, K., Meek, M. and Miller, J. (1992) *New Readings: Contributions to an Understanding of Literacy*, London: A & C Black.

Lancy, D. and Hayes, B. (1988) 'Interactive fiction and the reluctant reader', *English Journal*, **77**(7): 42–6.

Lanham, R. (1995) *The Electronic Word*, Chicago: Chicago Press.

Littleton, K., Selinger, M. and Kirkwood, A. (1998) 'Access to the Internet in a primary school: findings from the Educational Internet Service Providers (EISP) project', paper presented to the CEDAR conference, Warwick University, March 1998.

Loveless, A. (1995) *The Role of IT: Practical Issues for the Primary Teacher*, London: Cassell.

Meek, M. (1991) *On Being Literate*, London: The Bodley Head.

Miller, L., Blackstock, J. and Miller, R. (1994) 'An exploratory study into the use of CD-ROM storybooks', *Computers and Education*, **22**(1/2), 187–204.

Montague, M. M. (1990) *Computers, Cognition and Writing*, New York: State University of New York Press.

Papert, S. (1993) *The Children's Machine: Rethinking School in the Age of the Computer*, New York: Basic Books.

Perkins, J. and Newman, K. (1995) 'E-discourse in education', in D. T. Tinsley and T. J. van Weert (eds) *World Conference on Computers in Education VI: WCCE '95, Liberating the Learner*, London: Chapman Hall.

Ring, G., Ellis, R. and Reeves, T. (1994) 'Mental models, research and human computer interface design', *Second Interactive Multimedia Symposium*, Perth, Western Australia, 23–8 January, Promaco Conventions, Applecross.

Roblyer, M. D., Castine, W. H. and King, F. J. (1988) *Assessing the Impact of Computer-based Instruction: A Review of Research*, New York: Haworth Press.

Scrimshaw, P. (1993) 'Co-operative writing with computers', in P. Scrimshaw (ed.) *Language, Classrooms and Computers*, London: Routledge.

Snyder, I. A. (1994a) 'Writing with word processors: A research overview', *Journal of Curriculum Studies*, **26**: 43–62.

Snyder, I. A. (1994b) 'Teaching and learning writing with computers', in M. Wild and D. Kirkpatrick (eds) *Computer Education: New Perspectives*, Perth MASTEC, **26**. Edith Cowan University.

Woolley, B. (1993) *Virtual Worlds*, London: Penguin.

Chapter 2

Communicating Meaning –
Reading and Writing in a Multimedia World

Angela McFarlane

In the context of a multimedia world reading and writing are not restricted to the mere coding and decoding of text, rather they are being used to describe the processes of extracting meaning from, and recording and presenting your own meaning through, the full range of media. This would include the ability to manipulate the basic tools required to create and access these media, just as holding a pen, forming letters and turning pages are part of text-based literacy. The end products of literacy can range from a note to the milkman, to a hypertext on the Romans to a feature film. The common thread is that an author or group of authors have an idea or set of ideas which they wish to present to an audience. The audience will then extract a meaning or set of meanings from that presentation – which may or may not be the same as those the author(s) intended!

Until about 150 years ago the only commonly, but by no means universally, available means to engage in the process of communication of meaning was through text or static images either in two or three dimensions. These genres were well established with printed text having been in place for some 400 years. The form of writing had, however, been in continual evolution with spelling becoming standardized only in the nineteenth century; the novel as we know it a relatively modern addition. Over the last 150 years the number of genres available for both personal and mass communications have grown exponentially. These have included new media, such as photography and film, as well as new ways of creating established media, such as word processing and computerized painting tools. These changes have had an enormous impact on the ways we can express ideas and the size of the audiences that can be reached. Until the 1990s these new media were the preserve of a select few. Photographers and film-makers, recording artists and novelists formed an intellectual elite, the most successful of whom were and continue to be very well rewarded.

Until 1960, all these media had one thing in common – the format at least had a beginning, a middle and an end. Then Ted Nelson developed the idea of hypertext – a non-linear way of arranging material in 'chunks' with links between them. The hypertext author can create links between a set of ideas or information in an order which makes sense to them, but a reader is free to access these sets in an order of their own choosing. In this way the reader becomes co-author of the text they actually read.

None of these ideas, media or genres are less than 40 years old, so why the interest and attention now? A simple answer is access. The invention and affordability of the multimedia personal computer put ownership within the grasp of a wider population. This facilitates widescale access to create text, newsletters, books, edited video and mixed sound. Users of the computer also have access to sources of other people's creativity which they can read or edit into their own set of meaning and the Internet can be used to offer ideas to an audience of millions worldwide.

IMPLICATIONS FOR LITERACY

What does it mean to be literate, to be an active reader and writer, a communicator of meaning at the start of the twenty-first century? We are offered one, very well-defined view of literacy in the current government's literacy strategy. This deals almost exclusively with the use of printed texts. There are sixteen references to IT (Information Technology) in the whole five-year strategy – six of these to 'spell checkers', only one to non-linear texts and the rest to issues of layout such as the use of bullet points. Can the ability to spell 'accommodate', recognize a subordinate clause and write a Clerihew constitute being literate in today's world?

Assuming that text and its 'correct' usage is so important that it merits an hour a day for five years of compulsory schooling, why does the use of ICT for reading and producing text warrant such a low status, especially when those who work with the production of text do so almost exclusively through the use of computers? Professional writers use word processors because it is difficult to communicate meaning clearly and accurately at the first attempt. The process involves, at least at some level, drafting and redrafting. Text is regarded as a mutable entity, to be edited, added to and changed until it says exactly what the author wants it to say. This process of improving text is rare in schools where factors such as time and resources mean that teachers often end up settling for a child's first draft. As a result the whole purpose of the writing may be lost. The main reason that children are asked to write is to express themselves with clarity to others, communicate what they think, believe, know or feel about the subject of their writing and then to keep a record of it. The use of a word processor makes a dynamic approach to children's production of text a possibility. However, although word processing is the most common application in schools, the fullest potential of computers remains unexploited. So even if we accept the National Literacy Strategy's definition of literacy, this does not explain the absence of IT at the heart of the writing process (for a more detailed discussion of this issue see McFarlane 1997).

Perhaps the failure to recognize the importance of the computer in the creation and manipulation of text is symptomatic of a wider failure to admit the importance of twenty-first-century technology to modern literacy. This is a surprising but understandable – even perhaps inevitable – result of current attitudes to education. We live in a culture which at the policy level values quantifiable education, where results can be compared year on year, from school to school, from authority to authority. The problem with a view of literacy which embraces multiple media, and hypermedia, is that we do not have agreed definitions of these literacies, never mind a scale of measures of competence. While we can produce a detailed analysis of competence with written text, it seems difficult to produce definitions of competence with other media.

Furthermore, educators are not always competent in the use of multiple and hypermedia. Every teacher can read and write text to at least a moderate standard or they would not have been admitted to the profession. However, not all teachers can draw or paint, write or play music, compose hypermedia or even use a computer to access the Internet. This lack of personal literacy may partly account for the failure of some of them to recognize the value of these literacies. After all, most film goers would not be able to name a mid-shot or be able to articulate the significance of a cut versus a fade, yet they can still extract meaning from the genre. We neither know how to value visual media, nor are we very good at assessing collaborative effort. We know little of the process so we are left making our judgements on the basis of the product. And those judgements are largely subjective as we lack the knowledge and experience to define objective criteria.

Whatever the reasons, we are left failing to admit in school that the media children engage with out of school have value. In Britain the National Literacy Strategy is in danger of killing media education in primary schools and relegating the 'texts' of popular culture to the sidelines. This is true of established media such as television, magazines, song lyrics and film. It is hardly surprising then that it is also true of the newest digital media. The result is that we leave our children in a sea of meaning with no guidance as to the value, reliability or moral worth of the experiences they have there.

THE HOME EXPERIENCE

The popular view is that large numbers of children have access to computers at home. Estimates range from around 35 to 80 per cent of the current school population. It is of course a very difficult statistic to pin down. The DfEE is currently concerned that a gulf has opened between those children with home access and those without. The view is that children with a computer at home, especially where that computer has access to the Internet, will be greatly advantaged in terms of performance in the education system. Why this should be so is not articulated. As yet schools are not required to audit home ownership or access to a computer, even though they are urged to try and compensate those children without.

Computer-advantaged children will have access to a range of digital media and the tools to access and manipulate them. These will be extremely varied in terms of content and purpose. So much so that the fact that children are on a computer is almost the only common point of reference. Compare, for example, composing an e-mail letter to a friend, playing *Tomb Raider* and accessing the BBC Education website. Whatever they are doing, however, children will need, and be developing, literacies that go way beyond those in the National Literacy Strategy. They will also be having learning encounters which make a worksheet on the possessive pronoun even more soporific than it was before. Schools are hard pressed to keep up. Even the best resourced schools cannot always provide access to computers for children as and when it is appropriate. To do so the computer would have to be as available as the pencil case. If schools ever provided children with writing tools the practice was abandoned long ago – they must supply their own. Until children come to school with a powerful portable computer of their own, access will remain a key brake on the use of digital media in school. That day is still some way off, machines are still too expensive and too fragile and battery life remains short, although progress is impressive and sustained in all these areas. Even the £750 million being spent on the National Grid for Learning infrastructure until 2002 will not provide the required level of personal access.

THE CURRENT SITUATION

The current school culture is one which attaches great importance to neat handwriting and spelling, reading 'good' books and poetry and generally valuing the work of dead white men. The current home culture is one where all children watch TV and video and use the telephone and an increasing number access the Internet and use e-mail. And some children may read books. Given the importance of socio-economics in these areas the same children who have better access to computers are probably the ones with better access to books. Against this background one must ask how likely the National Literacy Strategy is to work. It is hard to see how the use of digital media to create meaning can find a place in the school day. Even extended writing is compromised. Where it does happen, in the form of multimedia authoring, there is a danger of an overemphasis on the processes rather than the outcomes. For example, if children are to create a multimedia presentation they will need to know how to create text, scan or draw images on screen and record sound. All of these skills must be taught to some degree. These processes are exciting, producing as they do a fast and powerful end product which is directly under the control of the child. It is tempting, especially where the teacher is inexperienced, to be so excited by the results that the usual critical faculties are suspended. The fact that a child has successfully captured an image and added text and sound to it can be judged at a number of levels. It may be that credit should be given for the manipulation of the hardware and software used or the fact that the author has succeeded in presenting these media together on one screen. However, critical appraisal must not stop there. There are issues of selection, relevance, originality, design and layout that should also be considered – both when teaching the topic and appraising the outcome. These are the process objectives associated with the creation of multimedia and include such skills as classifying information, building categories and developing connections.

Similarly when pupils are accessing multimedia as readers or, more accurately, co-authors as they select their routes through the materials teachers must not be blinded by their mere proficiency with the technology. It is not enough to be able to find a website or locate an image in *Encarta*, nor even to capture them. The information captured must be relevant to the questions that prompted the search. The end product must be well presented, incorporated into a presentation appropriately and with the required accreditation of the source.

A WAY FORWARD

So we are faced with a dilemma. Pupils enjoy a culture packed with media experiences that are under-represented in the school curriculum and not present at all in the formal assessment criteria which currently drive the school system. Moreover, those media experiences represent the ways of mass communication, now and in the future, where meaning is shared and messages are delivered. These are the media which will shape the children's views of themselves, the world around them and their place in it.

Perhaps we need to offer a way of describing and assessing the new literacies before the policy-makers will take us seriously. This is no easy task. As already mentioned it is impossible to find a universally accepted definition of visual literacy. However we already have a well-described and established set of definitions for the identification, analysis, selection and presentation of information. Perhaps this is a place to begin. This will not give us the full analysis of new literacies but perhaps we do not need that. What we do need is to build a value system that recognizes the new media and the skills needed to be literate in them; that is to convey and extract meaning.

I do not underestimate the culture change required if such a system is to be taken seriously in our schools. We currently have an emphasis on the easily assessed – not because it will achieve the declared ends of a more economically active population but largely because the assessment is achievable, at least practically. The skills that I am advocating cannot be assessed through paper and pencil tests. They require the ongoing analysis of a teacher who guides the learner and has a full perspective on a long-term piece of work as it evolves. In other words the system will have to begin to trust the judgement of teachers again.

Moreover, the majority of teachers do not currently have the skills needed to access or create multimedia, let alone judge the value of children's work. There is currently a unique training opportunity at hand: £230 million worth of in-service training for all practising teachers. There is an opportunity to embrace the new literacies and join the twenty-first century – do not throw it away on a word-processing course.

REFERENCES

Andresen, B. B. (1996) 'To be hypermedia-literate is to be liberated: reading, writing, arithmetic and hypermedia literacy as basic skills', *Educational Media International*, **33**(3): 110–13.

Bolter, J. D. (1991) *Writing Space: The Computer, Hypertext, and the History of Writing*, Hillsdale, N. J.; London: Lawrence Erlbaum Associates.

Bruce, B. C. (1997) 'Critical issues, literacy technologies: what stance should we take?', *Journal of Literacy Research*, **20**(2): 289–307.

Kinzer, C. and Leu, D. J. (1997) 'The challenge of change: exploring literacy and learning', in *Electronic Environments – Language Arts*, **74**: 126–36.

Kress, G. (1997) *Before Writing: Rethinking the Paths to Literacy*, London: Routledge.

McFarlane, A. (1997) 'Thinking about writing', in A. McFarlane (ed.) *Information Technology and Authentic Learning: Realising the Potential of Computers in the Primary Classroom*, London: Routledge.

Mitra, J. (1998) 'Creating multimedia texts: A new kind of publishing', *Language Matters* Spring: 16–18.

Plowman, L. (1998) 'Reading multimedia texts: Learning how CD-ROM texts work', *Language Matters* Spring: 19–22.

Reinking, D., Labbo, L., McKenna, M. and Kieffer, R. (eds) (1998) *Handbook of Literacy and Technology: Transformations in a Post-Typographic World*, Mahwah, N. J.; London: Lawrence Erlbaum Associates.

Robinson, M. (1997) *Children Reading Print and Television*, London; Washington D.C.: Falmer Press.

Tierney, R. J., Kieffer, R., Whalin, K., Desai, L., Moss, A. G., Harris, J. E. and Hopper, J. (1999) 'Assessing the impact of hypertext on learners' architecture of literacy learning spaces in different disciplines: Follow-up studies' http://www.readingonline.org/research/impact/tierhome.htm.

Chapter 3

Skills for Life:
New Meanings and Values for Literacies

Grace Kempster

This chapter asserts that the challenge for the new millennium is the reinvention of education. Unless education and its meanings blossom into learning then frankly it will not survive. These are exciting times where the bounds of formal education are overspilling. Whichever current sector we work in, there is a revolution where the learner is leading and old formulas of learning by rote or from elders are being turned upside down.

It is a disquieting experience watching young people with technology. They use it with familiarity and without thought, without the hype or hypertension of other age groups. They know exactly what they want and seek knowledge whether it is text or a still or moving image. Much reference is made in America to something called mediacy – literacy applied to all media – being able to read the text and the image and the moving image and the ability to secure understanding through reading the pictures as well as text in a rich and organic way.

The power of new technologies lies in the way in which they mirror the organic and messy nature of human learning and thought. It is likely that the readers of this book use word processing without thought. In writing this chapter, I did not begin at the beginning but started at the end, weaving the threads through afterwards, cutting and pasting, dotting about like a painter or artist – mirroring the human mind where thought evolves and develops in non-linear ways.

What I see when I see a child at a computer is a seamlessness between the way their young unfettered mind works and the glorious muddle of the Internet with its hot links, relational databases and data mining filled with dead ends, discoveries and things not yet understood.

Some may think it audacious for a professional librarian to comment on the future of education but I would contend that libraries have always been in the education business. They facilitate education for all those who have aged beyond the reach of teachers and act as the university for the under fives. They provide opportunities for self-directed learning in the locality. Children do not talk much about their library use. It is unmarked by exception, part of the fabric of their daily lives. The evidence is with us: the growth of library use by children has increased by 20 per cent over the last 10 years, making up 28 per cent of the library market now.

In the summer of 1999 Essex Library Service ran the annual *Big Summer Read* and the number of children taking part doubled across the county. Some 30,600 children aged 2–12 read, enjoyed and talked about 120,000 books to staff – all in a context of freedom to choose, to join in, to learn because it is fun, interesting or inspiring.

Research found that 86 per cent of teachers found the *Big Summer Read* had a tangible impact on maintaining or improving literacy levels among children. Libraries are the place where parents and carers, alienated or lacking confidence about approaching schools ask about reading problems and how they can help their child to learn. Be assured that libraries are not only used by reading-confident successful children. The atmosphere, approach and diversity of use and provision – the anonymity – is fiercely attractive to all, crossing socio-economic boundaries.

When the public library service established online@leeds, teachers queried why centres with homework librarians were needed in both schools and libraries. The evidence of regular use by children in their communities was there but some just found it hard to believe that so many children from so many schools found haven in their local library. The evidence of the achievement of the year's targets in the first three months of the project amazed the sceptics. We all have partial views of a child's world – joining them together will create confident and seamless environments for learning.

In 1992, the Youth Libraries group held a national conference with the title I have chosen for this chapter *Skills for Life: New Meanings and Values of Literacy*. It covered all forms of literacy: aural, computer, the content of media education, the needs of the child with disabilities and the multicultural dimension – in reflecting on the conclusions of that conference there are many resonances today. The vital nature of library services to the under fives where the seeds of literacy are sown is celebrated with the many Bookstart initiatives across the country. Books and reading *are* for babies. Literacy is a means not an end in itself and experiences at the youngest age foster the drive and desire to acquire, practise and retain this vital skill for life. Some experts suggest 50 per cent of a child's learning potential is developed before they are five years old.

The advent of the National Literacy Strategy and the Literacy Hour may have inspired many worried parents. It was in the media and on their minds. Their concern was that whatever their own life chances, their children would have a better start in the educational stakes. Libraries have never been about books, contrary to their physical emanations. They have always been about reading experiences and impact. A young library reader expressed the fundamentals better than any librarian could when saying, 'My library's like a lighthouse – it illuminates my mind . . .'

And in that freedom to find out, be delighted and discover, meeting through the intimate pages of a book, authors and illustrators living and long dead, we all experience something tangible and virtual – connection and understanding beyond the bounds of the realistic. We connect, we seek to understand and be understood. In her novel *Impossible Saints* (1997), Michèle Roberts describes well this basic human need and right, a truly felt need and hunger. But this need is not only fed by imaginative literature; readers bring inspiration, facts and a host of assumptions to any reading experience. Books are not complete without the reader – why else do we react so diversely and differently when sharing our reading experiences? We leave pieces of ourselves between the book covers and reveal ourselves, our situations and places in understanding and development.

So why is library use by the young blossoming and growing? Is it because of failures in formal education? For some the answer must be yes. The straitjacket of educational achievement and narrow pathways to success mean that early disenchantment sets in, bringing alienation. However that is not the only answer. For others the library is a place of freedom, finding out and reading beyond the narrow bounds of the National Curriculum. A place and space that is unfettered by judgements, where you make the choice to spend time, waste time, dip into the difficult and the different, where you can extend and deepen your learning and extend your educational success.

One uniqueness of libraries is their strength in diversity of meanings and values. They are not confined by one function but can and do hold a cornucopia of purpose for a diversity of people.

Another uniqueness of libraries lies in the combinations they make – people do read fact with fiction, poems with biography and that choice in one place makes them powerful connectors in joining up learning. We must move on from the Books v. Technology debate – it is tedious and dated – we need to return to the meanings and values of the reading experience whether page or screen, image or text.

In July 1997 the Library and Information Commission published a ground-breaking report called *New Library: the People's Network*. It was seminal for many reasons, not least because it presented government with solutions to joining up learning across the nation by looking at the content, connectivity and competencies needed to translate the meanings and values of libraries in the electronic age. Its vision will be realized – a public library network with connections to the National Grid for Learning, a service operating in virtual and actual worlds simultaneously, offering technology with the human touch. It is the blueprint for library development and will impact on the lives and opportunities of everyone.

Think for a moment what this means for you in your work and life – an opportunity or a threat? Library staff are also being trained from NOF (New Opportunities Fund) funds with the aim of everyone becoming confident and competent in using ICT. There will also be specialists with advanced training as IT Managers, Net Navigators and Educators. There is a real opportunity in the interests of the learner to merge the teaching and library professions, the uniqueness of teachers transformed into learning facilitators and on offer to all despite the tyranny of distance.

You may think that this is a David and Goliath situation – formal education is vast and public libraries relatively minor – but you know what happened in that particular story! Just because libraries and schools have existed for 150 years does not give either the inalienable right to continue in existing shapes and forms. The two areas need each other. Children spend so little of their lives in school – to achieve the educational targets rigorously and clearly set by the government, the need exists to create a complementary, not contradictory, landscape either side of the formal learning day and to think in new ways about learning. Children learn in schools because they have to – they learn in libraries because they want to. The urge to know, understand and enjoy is the real stimulus for literacy.

This chapter began with the contention that what we speak of now is a new mediacy. That holds threats as the confines of the sequential page are blown apart. Yet within that format the very young are to be found reading the pictures. You cannot know about the fox in *Rosie's Walk* unless you read the pictures; like many picture books the whole experience is intermingled and deeply satisfying. It is also liberating for many children as their critical faculties are extended in a multimedia participative environment.

Could it be that the threat we all feel is that with the learner leading, it is unclear where the power lies? Stephen Heppell's vision of the future is one where the role of the teacher turned learning facilitator becomes one of tool kit provider for the learning journey; providing a tool kit of skills for use on ipsitive learning journeys, as well as markers of progress and development. In this there is a real convergence of purpose. Librarians have long been concerned about information handling skills enabling people to make their own judgements and choices – education with a light touch; expertise in assaying information and offering choices, all neutral, highly skilled and tempered with non-invasive interpersonal skills – and totally on the side of the learner. New alliances must be formed to deliver real learning, not competing but connecting and complementing.

Teachers no longer have inalienable rights to control learning, because the learner is in charge and will make choices. The pick and mix learning of the next century will widen the gap between those who have daily use of books with technology in the home and those who do not. Libraries are the solution not the problem and unless we all work together in win-win alliances the threat is that the learning disadvantaged will upset the applecart of prosperity for us all.

The agenda is transforming information into knowledge in the hope that this leads to understanding, tolerance and fulfilment for all. The danger is that the next generation will operate more effectively in the virtual rather than the real world, cocooned as they are in bedrooms across the country and able, unlike life, to turn it off if control is lost. Computer access and expertise is becoming a badge of status and success; a new social class is emerging which is clearly defined by whether one has easy access to the revolution behind closed screens or not, where the relationship to the flashing cursor means more than the relationship with people.

It is a bitter-sweet revolution with wonders and woes. The hope is that when we look back at the latter half of the last century we did not miss the chance to connect – to influence together and to make a real difference to the lives of all, to join up thinking.

Library services across the country are fitting themselves for the future – not just in upskilling to use ICT but to develop expertise in education and lifelong learning, creating, if they do not already have them, children's specialists, learning specialists, information choreographers and reader-development roles for key staff. Being a librarian will never be the same again, with excitement, energy and enthusiasm unleashed among many. Public libraries want to be wired up not because it is cool or fashionable but because they know what to do with technology and will be as effective in organizing and assaying information and imagination in the electronic age as they are in the actual age. The role of the library is fundamentally the same in both ages: powerful connectors for learning and understanding in an increasingly complex and hybrid environment.

In researching for this chapter, I found that while there is much coverage of the wiring up of other nations for the Information Age, in particular Singapore and America, there is in fact little current research in public libraries' ICT provision and its management for children (Denham *et al.*, 1997). I know that much of the current development is happening so fast that authoritative evaluation is not yet in place but it needs to be.

There is a blossoming of websites which are both imaginative and participative such as the virtual world of Stories on the Web to the singularly zany Fiction Cafe for blind teenagers which speaks your dishes of the day. In Essex, there are CD-ROMs targeted for homework support in all 74 libraries, with the New Library Network ensuring 10 Internet connections in small libraries and 40 in medium to large ones, all linked to the National Grid for Learning. Homework clubs are increasingly being successfully established in libraries although the NOF guidelines make that process complicated. Public libraries do not have a problem in working with local schools but they are frustrated by the lack of forward thinking to recognize them as obvious places for out of hours learning – open and most used at weekends and during school holidays.

The exciting aspect is the way enabling technologies can engender respect and acknowledgement of other literacies, especially for the oral tradition of storytelling of no less value in an attempt to communicate than the written word. One comment from Desmond Spiers, himself profoundly deaf, expresses the feelings of many: 'Unless you can speak, you are not considered literate.' I love the anonymity and egalitarianism of the Internet – no one knows you are deaf on e-mail – for many it is truly liberating.

Finally and fundamentally, literacies have to be about power and are entwined with one's identity, true expression. This is a momentous time; there has never before been such potential for the liberating impact of literacies and potency of threat for those without the threshold literacies. The focus of libraries clearly is on the motivation to read and the stimulus to continue to practise the skills of literacy across all media.

REFERENCES

Barker, K. and Lonsdale, R. (eds) (1992) 'Skills for life? The meaning and value of literacy', London: Graham Taylor, *Proceedings of the Youth Libraries Group Conference*, September 1992.

Denham, D., Nankivell, C. and Elkin, J. (1997) *Children and IT in public libraries: a research project*, Birmingham: UCE.

Hutchins, P. (1968) *Rosie's Walk*, London: The Bodley Head.

Library and Information Commission (1997) *New Library: The People's Network*, London: LIC.

Library and Information Commission (1998) *Building the New Library Network*, London: LIC.

Roberts, M. (1997) *Impossible Saints*, London: Little Brown.

Taylor, G. (1993) *Youth Library Review*, Spring 1997: 20–9.

Part Two

APPLICATIONS

Chapter 4

A New Relationship with Media?

Richard Millwood

INTRODUCTION

Much has been made of the advent of the twenty-first century and the technological advances that have come before it and will no doubt continue. As business, education and wider society has rushed to embrace that most sophisticated of tools, the general purpose computer, it is necessary to pose the question: how will teaching and learning be affected by new modes of communication, new tools for expression and new ways for the representation of knowledge? This chapter focuses on a model of 'micro-learning' – the basic, everyday behaviour that drives human learning, which in turn provides a framework to consider ways in which ICT might transform learning through the computer as a tool for the creative learner.

KNOWLEDGE AND PURPOSE

The assumptions driving this discussion are as follows:

1. That individuals rely on mental models in order to know and to do – even for simple acts like recalling facts. Such models may be held consciously as well as unconsciously, are informal and faulty, and may be revealed to an individual through introspection or to others through patterns of behaviour and discussion.
2. That there is an external, recorded body of shared knowledge in the form of oral and performance tradition, books, film and television and other media (particularly World Wide Web) which represents accepted and disputed meanings in society.
3. To become familiar with subsets of this recorded knowledge through adaptation of internal mental models already constructed from infant experience (particularly models of the physical world, the social and

interpersonal world and the world of language) is a central, empowering purpose for the learning individual.

4. Questioning, doubting and re-expressing this knowledge is fundamental to a high-quality learning process.

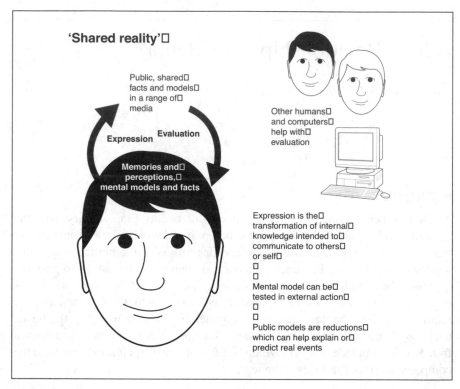

Figure 4.1: Internal and external knowledge

These assumptions drive a model of learning which I believe can inform practice and justify decisions about deployment of ICT. Without such a model, there is a tendency to take an over-pragmatic view of what works with computers and to sustain practices and decisions justified on past success with older, poorer designed technology and software in a social, cultural and technological context which has moved on. What is needed is some principle to base decisions on.

MICRO-LEARNING, EXPRESSION AND EVALUATION

Micro-learning is a term used to describe the day-to-day, minute-by-minute processes which lead to more secure knowledge for the learner. In Figure 4.1 expression and evaluation are linked in a feedback loop which drives understanding and performance.

Figure 4.2 shows a partial model of learning which indicates the relationship between expression and evaluation. This behaviour can be observed in the learning process when children are tackling problems and discussing solutions at operational, content and overview levels. For example, in the context of working with computers to assemble a multimedia presentation, learners might insert a sound or video clip and then view the results of their work to evaluate whether their understanding of the tool was correct and whether the insertions were correct in terms of content or placement in the sequence. They might then evaluate the presentation to identify whether they had achieved their original intention to communicate their concepts to an audience. It is an iterative process, a loop going round and round between the formulation of ideas and the testing of their validity, which can be described as an engine driving the learning process at many levels.

Young children in groups can be observed engaged in this kind of discussion all the time, arguably an indicator that learning is taking place.

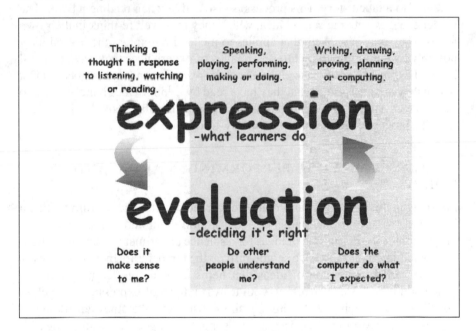

Figure 4.2: Modes of expression and questions for evaluation

Expression can be divided up into three categories:

1. Internal expression (based on thought);
2. Speaking, playing, performing, making and doing (based on direct 'real time' action);
3. Formal expression (based on recorded and/or symbolic forms).

INTERNAL EXPRESSION

This involves what is going on internally, in one's mind, in response to a listening, watching or reading activity. For example, if a teacher is talking and a child is listening, the internal expressive act is what the child is doing in their head. They are thinking in response to what is being said, if they are 'on theme' (which they needn't be – they may be thinking about last night's television or what they are going to do at football after school, in which case they won't be learning what the teacher wants). If they are 'on task', then they are probably re-expressing in thought what the teacher has said, as far as they possibly can, in order to try and make sense of it. They may be asking the question 'Does it make sense to me?' or even 'Would it make sense to others?'

The same cycle of expression and evaluation can continue while, for example, watching a television programme, using a multimedia CD-ROM or listening to a taped story. This process is also active when reading a book. The reader engages with the central idea, which they may well re-think in their own terms. They may say 'Well, that applies to me' and re-express the central idea, possibly by conjuring up pictures or images of experiences they have had. All kinds of expressions may take place inside the reader's head as thoughts, against which they are measuring what they have read by asking 'Does it make sense to me?', 'Does it match up with what I think is going on in this book?' This internal learning process continues throughout day-to-day life.

SPEAKING, PLAYING, PERFORMING, MAKING AND DOING

Speaking in this context is particularly concerned with the idea of formulating a hypothesis to an informal audience – the notion of 'thinking out loud'. This might include the discussion of ideas for a science experiment, where one might say something like 'I think we should turn up the temperature by five degrees' – it is the verbal expression of ideas that helps to focus the learning process. 'Playing' in the sense of working with toys is a form of expression. The child tests ideas by playing and thinking about whether what they are doing is appropriate. 'Performing' as in a play or a song, 'making' as in constructing a kit or 'doing' in the more general sense of engaging in outward activity, such as a game of football, are expressive acts which involve continuous evaluation and re-assessment. The expressions are often replayed, respoken and reperformed until the learner feels that they are right. This is not just a mental process – now the evaluations and judgements of others inform the process. The learner considers, 'Do other people understand me?' in addition to their own thoughts.

This additional tool to feed the learning loop has great power, because others may take more objective views, by which I mean their views may be less driven by affect because they may have more experience and knowledge by which to evaluate your performance. Teachers are particularly well placed here because they hone their evaluative remarks based on experience of other children's mistakes. Indeed it is their understanding of partial failure and repair (situated advice about improving performance) which makes teachers such significant supports for the learning process.

FORMAL EXPRESSION

Formal expression includes processes such as writing, drawing, proving, planning and computing. Formal expression is also recorded, for later 'asynchronous' evaluation, on paper, audio tape, video tape or computer file. It is formal in the sense that the learner is attempting to use some kind of language, which is more constrained and rule-governed than the unrestricted thought, performance or speech process. For instance, the formal writing process includes the rules and conventions of written grammar and vocabulary, structural form and page layout. Diagrammatic drawings follow conventions (not always well explained or understood) and to take the ultimate formality of a computer expression, for example in spreadsheets, the information is arranged in strict tabular form using formulae which must be syntactically correct to function at all, unlike ordinary human discourse.

This formal nature, although challenging, is desirable if the expression is to be successfully communicated to others, or indeed through a computer. In some cases it becomes essential if the computer is to perform at all. For example, when constructing a Web page using HTML (Hypertext Mark-up Language, the language of the World Wide Web), a simple missing bracket can lead to overall failure. Nevertheless the benefit of such computer-based expressions is that they continue to respond to the same kind of evaluations as before, i.e. 'Does it make sense to me?', 'Do other people understand me?', but now a further question can be added, 'Does the computer do what I expected?'

An example of this can be observed when using the programming language Logo to draw a triangle by defining the actions of an imaginary or real robot. Learners often write the program:

FORWARD 100

RIGHT 60

FORWARD 100

RIGHT 60

FORWARD 100

Which leads to the following shape:

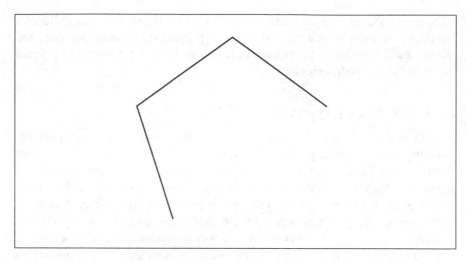

Figure 4.3: A 'buggy' triangle program creates a non-triangle!

Many teachers have seen children (and adults) make this mistake. Of course the angle to turn right should be 120 degrees rather than 60 degrees (in the program, RIGHT 120 instead of RIGHT 60) and the learner can achieve that through trial and error with feedback from the resultant shape until they are satisfied.

The learner has not had the feedback 'No, you got it wrong'. The learner can evaluate their expression, with the evidence of their own eyes, because the computer has drawn the triangle they expected. This is what Seymour Papert termed 'debugging', where correcting program errors is seen as an essential part of the learning process (Papert, 1980).

The important point here is that the computer does not actually assess the student. It simply performs what they have told it to do and in doing so has no concept of triangle, learning or purpose. The computer has not superseded the teacher but it has provided a reflective mechanism for the learner to evaluate formal expressions.

This model helps to articulate reasons for using a computer as a creative, communicative and expressive tool rather than the more simplistic 'computer as teacher and information provider' role. It is disheartening to see how often governments, policy-makers, educationalists and many others miss the point about how children can benefit from using computers for the lack of a meaningful and pragmatic model of learning.

NOISY CLASSROOMS CAN BE PRODUCTIVE CLASSROOMS

If one accepts this dynamic feedback loop as a driver of learning, then it might help those who feel uncomfortable about noisy classrooms. In such classrooms children are often discussing social matters, the television they saw last night, gossip about peers and their interests. Although this seems 'off task', what it achieves is a sense of ease and relaxation among the children to express 'on task' ideas, which in a less friendly context risk derision.

If all were silent, it would prevent evaluation, except in thought. A noisy classroom not only gives learners the licence to express ideas, it also means that others have the chance to provide evaluation. Other people's understanding of an expression is as crucial as knowing whether the expression is right. Another child saying; 'I get you' (meaning I understand your expression) can be as powerful for learning as a teacher saying: 'That's the right answer.'

The hunger for this kind of evaluation is evident in the following extract from a transcript made from a video of three children playing *Droidworks*, a three-dimensional virtual reality game centred around a *Star Wars* theme which encourages informal problem-solving in a scientific context.

Patrick: I'll die if I go down there!
Sasha: Like getting damaged. Getting all the way damaged do you mean? Getting damaged.
Sasha: Do you know when you die? You die when you get all damaged, is what it means, when it all gets red or the green turns into red.
Sasha: The red is damage and the green isn't damage. Do you understand?
Sasha: When you get all damaged then you die.
Sasha: Is that right Patrick?
Patrick: Yes, yeh that's right.

Sasha is verbally expressing himself about the meaning of the symbols on the screen to do with the status of the robot, how damaged it is and what it means to die as a robot. This is not a philosophical argument, this is interpreting what's going on in the computer program. In the full transcript, he seeks confirmation of his ideas over and over again, slightly clarifying his words to articulate his theories better, and seeking evaluation from Patrick, almost driving him to distraction! Needless to say, Patrick who is older, shows his care for Sasha by patiently agreeing with his ideas – they have a relationship which can withstand the repetitiveness of the experience.

At the same time, Patrick is expressing himself in this dialogue by his control and navigation of the virtual robot; the others are evaluating his expressions by watching his performance on the screen and occasionally commenting or guiding him.

HOW THE COMPUTER CAN SUPPORT EXPRESSION AND EVALUATION

From time to time events occur in the *Droidworks* program, as the children play with it, which confirm or deny their hypotheses – an experience which can be observed when using almost any simulation software. Note that the computer does not evaluate the children's expressions directly but simply responds according to the simulation's model and the user's inputs. It is the children who evaluate on the basis of the screen feedback and their own expectations – they judge for themselves and each other how right or wrong they were with their hypotheses.

The same kind of experience can be observed with electronic educational toys like the Pixie. Sasha wants the Pixie to make 'steps' – a staircase pattern of right angles. He expresses this pattern by pressing the forward and left and right buttons on the Pixie in an appropriate sequence. The Pixie constrains his expression – it is impossible to make a syntactic error, since the formal language is embodied in the keys on the top of the Pixie, unlike the Logo earlier, where it is all too easy to misspell or incorrectly arrange keywords and values. So Sasha is helped in his expression by the simplicity of the toy. He evaluates his expression by watching the Pixie perform – he can see its behaviour and decide whether he programmed it correctly by his own targets and judgements.

TIMELINESS AND QUALITY

Not all evaluation needs to be immediate. In the case of confirming facts, such as with learning the times tables (number bond facts), it helps to have immediate feedback on your expressions. However, if you are recording your expression, for example in writing an essay or drawing a picture, then feedback can be given later since it is so easy to revisit the expression. When the learner comes to read the marks and the comments that the teacher (or peer) has made beside them, there's a sense in which they can locate the two together and launch back into re-expressing, correcting ideas and improving them.

Far more important than timeliness is the question of quality. The number one

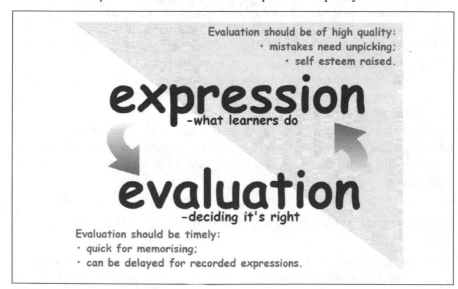

Figure 4.4: Quality and timeliness in evaluation

thing about learning is that mistakes need 'unpicking'. It is possible to improve on mistakes simply by knowing that they are right or wrong but it is far more productive to be told in what way they are wrong. This kind of evaluation demands experience and knowledge about the mistakes learners in general make and a knowledge of the individual making the mistake – a capacity that good teachers have but computers do not. The other thing that teachers must do, of course, is to raise self-esteem in the process. Learners are going to fail. Every learner is going to fail repeatedly. If they didn't fail they wouldn't be learners – one fails and learns through failure. That sounds awfully negative but it isn't, because the failure is usually only partial and much of what learners express is close to the mark. Nevertheless, it is a failure of a kind and as a result evaluation must reinforce self-esteem as well as unpick errors. It is arguably the case that if children's self-esteem is not at a high enough level, they will reject learning. They will reject the expression and evaluation loop. They will not be in a loop; they will be out of the loop. There is evidence that success in secondary school is highly dependent on the self-esteem children have in primary education. Computer software can help in evaluation by delightful behaviour which makes the use of even drill and practice software fun and rewarding. Computers also help with self-esteem in the expression of ideas by making the production of expressions in a form and at quality levels which match those of the rest of the world. Learners can print at the same quality level as books and even make film which in quality terms matches the Hollywood production. In neither case does the computer strongly support the quality of content but at least this is the area that can be focused on rather than the self-disgust induced by poor handwriting which in so many cases leads to rejection.

EXPRESSIVE TOOLS MATTER!

The point about expounding on learning as an expressive and evaluative act in an iterative loop, a revisited loop that goes on throughout one's life, is to say that expression matters. It matters that you can express yourself and it matters that you can express yourself well because expression acts as part of that engine to learn in the first place. And that's why literacy matters. If you take literacy in its simplest sense – the collection of abilities to understand others and to articulate ideas and communicate them – then it is the central platform for learning of all kinds. The central expressive medium in education is, of course, recorded text – writing and reading.

However, computers are changing this orthodoxy. As well as reading and writing, we now have spreadsheets, diagrams, digital video and photography, animation, digital sound and hypertexts – all of these new recorded media. Moreover, the tools to revise expressions in these media are now available, user friendly and thus the cost of revising expressions is low. 'Writing' a video essay or a hypertext project report is now eminently achievable, as is a collage of audio or an animation of graphical data. These, and many other previously highly skilled, time-consuming and expensive forms, are now happily produced by young children, adolescents and adults with the support of good computer tools.

When we look at computers to ask 'What should we use them for?' it is entirely clear that if they are to support learning then they must support expression in the new media.

NEW MEDIA TOOLS – DIGITAL VIDEO EDITING

So how hard is it to express yourself in new digital media? Making digital video is not simply the capturing of events on a camcorder – as any film-maker will tell you, the editing process is what makes a film (and the layering of audio is probably equally significant).

The software that comes with the operating system can, in some cases, offer simple expressive tools in digital video editing. QuickTime, the technology that supports digital video on Apple and PC platforms, is such a tool. Using QuickTime Player, the skills required to create and modify a sequence of video material are no more than those of selection, cutting and pasting – conceptually familiar terms in many users' repertoire, based on word-processing experience. Even the keyboard shortcuts and menu commands are the same, although the media being manipulated are different in nature.

Transferring video media from the latest DV (Digital Video) camcorders into computers is easy and structured – the software (Apple's iMovie, for example) separates the sequences into pieces based on the shots taken automatically, ready for selection, editing and sequencing. Visual timelines show the results of your

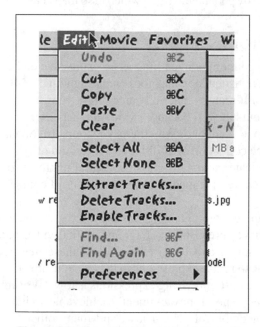

Figure 4.5: The Edit menu in QuickTime Player

editing decisions and support your plans for telling a story in the same way as an outliner can in a word processor.

If children could create their essays as videos instead of writing them, they might avoid the challenges connected with the symbol-centred medium of text (knowing how the symbols work, knowing how the spelling and grammar works). The grammars of television may be more familiar for a child or simply preferred stylistically. It would be hard for us then to deny digital video as a choice of means of expression (and thus learning).

Some of the barriers to making this choice an option include access to equipment, formal assessment criteria and teacher experience. The equipment is already in place or on its way – the general purpose multimedia computer. The formal assessment criteria will be much harder to address, in part because of the third barrier. Few teachers and even fewer headteachers, inspectors and examination markers will have a lifetime of experience in digital video as a medium of expression, unlike their experience of text. Educationalists are particularly textually literate (that's why they have been successful) but they have not had the opportunities presented by cheap digital video editing.

NEW MEDIA TOOLS – HYPERTEXT

At least digital video has roots in the film and television world, which has a century or more of tradition and development. Hypertext has none of these advantages. We are only now making best use of this tool for mapping knowledge and making materials available in new juxtapositions.

Editors for making World-Wide-Web pages are readily available, often for free (for example Netscape Composer), but rarely do they offer overview of structure and manipulation of structure. In other words, to conceive of the hypertext as an interconnected network of Web pages takes imagination and the tools are not yet good at supporting this. The essential difference with hypertext as a new medium is the non-linear structure (what becomes of narrative?). Arguably, designing hypertext is closer to mind mapping and concept maps/mapping than it is to writing texts.

NEW MEDIA TOOLS – PANORAMAS

Another wholly new medium is the panorama. The panorama is an interactive medium, which allows the user to navigate a set of photographs which have been stitched together into a seamless 360-degree view of a scene. To make the panorama, the author takes about 18 photographs in a circle from a central point using a digital still camera, transfers the photographs to the computer and then uses panorama stitching software (for example Claris QuickTime, VR Authoring Studio or Photovista). The whole process can take as little as 15 minutes. Eight-year-old children are quite capable of managing the process and bring all kinds of imaginative ideas to the concept (boys have staged a fight scene!).

Figure 4.6: A portion of a panorama

Unlike ordinary photography, the product is not a fixed, pictorial composition – the creator does not determine the frame that the viewer may choose. Instead the scene as a whole is composed, ready for multiple views by the viewer. The opportunity to create rich views of scenes as an expressive act as well as the appreciation of scenes by viewers is novel and exciting for all concerned.

Common to all these media is a relinquishing of control by the author in favour of the viewer – the author must plan for alternatives and choices and not dominate the narrative.

CONCLUSION – A NEW RELATIONSHIP WITH MEDIA

The nature of these new media and the tools to produce them raise the question 'What is the nature of the new integrated media?' It is an unknown, evolving combination of flexible integration between familiar media and new tools for creation and viewing. Even technology experts are not as knowledgeable of these new media as the traditional forms – they are making sense of them later in life, not having grown up with them. Teachers certainly don't know about new media, even though they are considerably expert in their own right.

It is thus clear that there are new relationships to be forged, new places for digital media to occupy in the repertoire of learner and teacher. What we can do is judge the new forms of media by the contribution they make in adding richness and in giving a wide spectrum of choice for learners to express their ideas, in supporting that expression with helpful and powerful tools and in supporting the evaluation of expression with flexible viewing tools.

In this discussion there has been no place to consider the 'classroom' for this new expression and evaluation but the Internet is surely the place for sharing such ideas and communicating knowledge and will deliver opportunity for new authors and audiences through the emerging online communities.

REFERENCES

Bruner, J. S. (1966) *Toward a Theory of Instruction*, Cambridge, MA: Harvard University Press.

Hargreaves, D. H. (1975) *Interpersonal Relations and Education*, London: Routledge & Kegan Paul.

Lucas Learning (1998) *Star Wars: Droidworks*, CD-ROM.

Papert, S. (1980) *Mindstorms*, New York: Harvester Press.

Vygotsky, L. (1934) *Thought and Language*, Cambridge, MA: MIT Press.

Chapter 5

Electronic Communication in the Twenty-first-century Classroom

Nick Easingwood

The recent change in terminology from Information Technology (IT) to Information and Communications Technology (ICT) inspired by the Stevenson Report (1997) reflects a subtle yet distinct change in approach to what the use of the new technologies in our classrooms really means. The former term suggested that there was a one-way flow of information with the user being a passive recipient of material displayed on the screen. The adding of the word 'communication' implies a more dynamic interaction between the user and the world of information contained beyond the computer screen. As a result of this, the computer has evolved from being a teaching machine to being a tool to support learning and ultimately into a means of instigating communication from a local to global scale. Through information flow and feedback the computer has rapidly enhanced the capability of people to communicate over small or vast distances instantly and easily.

In October 1997 the appearance of the document *Connecting the Learning Society*, based on many of the recommendations of the Stevenson Report, heralded a revolution in our schools which will reverberate well into the twenty-first century. Although computers had been present in British schools in various states of repair and usage for about 15 years, this represented the first serious attempt to take a co-ordinated approach to providing hardware, software, materials and training for schools. The idea that all schools would be connected to the Internet by 2002 ensured that the three-year programme would have a sense of direction and urgency that hasn't always been associated with the British education system. According to page 3 of *Connecting the Learning Society*, the National Grid for Learning (NGfL), as it became known, ensured that 'a mosaic of inter-connecting networks and education services based on the Internet which will support teaching, learning, training and administration in schools, colleges, universities, libraries, the workplace and homes' developed quickly and effectively.

The very fact that all of these institutions have access to Internet facilities represents one of the most exciting and forward-thinking developments in the last 20 years. *Connecting the Learning Society* goes on to say that the Grid would '. . . provide a national focus and agenda for harnessing new technologies to raise educational standards, and to improve quality of life and Britain's international competitiveness, especially the new literacy and numeracy targets' (*op. cit.*, p. 3).

Then came new literacy and numeracy targets. However, a note of caution needs to be sounded here. How will the advent of the widespread use of new technologies sit with an educational climate that reinforces a 'traditional' approach to literacy and numeracy? Given that the National Literacy Strategy document only has sixteen rather narrow specific references to ICT, how can we as teachers and educationalists ensure that new technology supports a new literacy as well as an existing one? As there are so few specific references to ICT in the National Literacy Strategy (1998b), it comes as little surprise that some teachers are not incorporating ICT into their teaching. However, according to Barker and Franklin (1998), leaving ICT out of the Literacy Hour 'would be to do a disservice to an amazingly motivating and versatile tool'. They go on to suggest that in order to determine whether ICT is the most appropriate tool for an activity, teachers should go through the 'four E's'. Teachers should ask if ICT Eases and supports the task; Enables the learner; Ensures that the learning outcomes can be achieved and Enhances the task's quality and value. Barker and Franklin conclude that if ICT doesn't perform these functions, then it shouldn't be used. These criteria, of course, could just as easily apply to any area of the curriculum, not just literacy.

Bearing this in mind the requirements of *Connecting the Learning Society* are certainly not rhetoric. There is a clear and definite commitment to develop ICT in British schools which is reflected in a range of documents that were published in 1998. Government *Circular 4/98* entitled *Teaching: High Status, High Standards* (DfEE, 1998a), effectively a National Curriculum for Initial Teacher Training in England and Wales, overtly mentions e-mail in paragraph 12 of Section B of Annex B, the section that specifically refers to ICT in subject teaching. As far as serving teachers are concerned the New Opportunities Fund, which has made available £230 million of Lottery funding, will train all teachers to use computers with children by the year 2002. There is a clear expectation that teachers will use e-mail to communicate with each other as well as with 'experts' in particular fields of expertise. As Niki Davis (Somekh and Davis, 1997) argues, professional development can be improved through the use of ICT, especially when it enhances a teacher's learning. However, in order for pupils to use the technology effectively, the teachers themselves need to be trained to use ICT proficiently. The use of e-mail could act as a surreptitious means of developing staff not only in their ICT skills but also in other curriculum areas through e-mailing other teachers and experts.

In many ways the most exciting aspect of putting schools on line via the National Grid for Learning is not so much that it gives access to the material on the Internet but the corresponding use of electronic mail. The potential that this not so new technology offers children in our schools is enormous, offering as it does the ability to connect schools with libraries, museums and, of course, other individuals within the world at large. According to *Connecting the Learning Society* (1997) there are over 32,000 state and independent schools with over 9 million pupils and 450,000 teachers, 900 further education colleges with 4 million students and 250,000 staff, with 380,000 people employed in higher education containing 1.6 million students in the United Kingdom alone. Add to this 4,300 libraries employing 22,000 staff which are used by over 60 per cent of the adult population each year and other institutions such as museums and galleries – both in the UK and abroad – and the true scope of the potential of the NGfL alone becomes enormous. The intention that by 2002 75 per cent of teachers and lecturers and 50 per cent of pupils and students will have their own e-mail addresses via school reinforces this. The ability for children, teachers, librarians, museum officials and other educationalists to communicate with each other over a vast network represents one of the most exciting means of developing education at the start of the twenty-first century. ICT ensures that education and the real world meet in a context that can be used and enhanced both in and outside the classroom. The ability to contact any individual anywhere in the world is a powerful tool that we should not overlook.

So why has such a great emphasis been placed on the value of e-mail within our education system? Quite apart from the fact that ICT represented a major part of the pre-1997 election strategy of the Labour Party, it seems to have captured the imagination of a large part of the population. Why was ICT deemed such a good thing? Why was the e-mail target set? By a peculiar paradox, the introduction of widespread use of e-mail in our schools in many ways represents a regressive technology. Watching any old Western movie reinforces the notion that non-verbal communication by telegraph over wires across vast distances is by no means new. Indeed, as the American West was opened up during the nineteenth century the spread of the railroads drove a corresponding development in this primitive means of communication. The subsequent invention of the telephone ensured that individuals could have two-way conversations in real time, enabling information to be conveyed clearly and with expression. Subsequently the telegram, telex and, more recently, the fax machine has enabled text to be carried over a communications network that for the most part was developed to handle telephone calls. The supreme irony is that schools are investing in a technology that will use this network as a step forward – yet rarely have schools encouraged pupils or students to use the phone or fax to search for information in the same way that the NGfL does. Indeed, the computer keyboard itself is laid out in a similar way to a typewriter (remember those?), the QWERTY arrangement being carried over to the new technology so as not to de-skill several generations of experienced typists who had learned their trade in a previous era. Certainly e-mail is not in itself new; companies and the worldwide academic community have used it regularly for many years. It is the relatively recent widespread availability of ICT across all aspects of society that has brought about the innovation. Not only do most organizations and companies have websites – indeed there is great cache in having a Web address, particularly if it ends in .com, but also the individuals within have their own e-mail addresses, either at work or at home. Indeed, a new kind of status and accountability has been brought about by the use of e-mail. For example, some major national broadsheet newspapers now include the e-mail address of their journalists at the end of their columns. So now one can e-mail the individual concerned and discuss the content of the piece. Although it always was possible to directly contact such journalists by the more traditional technologies of letter, fax or telephone, the inclusion of an e-mail address makes the whole affair that much more interactive, that much more accountable.

One of the many advantages of using e-mail in school is that it represents an easy way into using a computer. Rather than learning how to use the computer in order to complete a given task, such as writing a letter on a word processor or setting up a spreadsheet to handle an account, the use of e-mail ensures that the user has to use the technology to access the communication network beyond. As a result, learning to use e-mail can act as a microcosm of learning to use the computer itself. In a presentation to the SEDA Conference at the University of Southampton during April 1998, Hamish MacLeod of the University of Edinburgh demonstrated that the introduction to new students of e-mail during induction periods significantly increased those individuals' ICT key skills. Likewise, getting teachers and pupils on-line will act as a catalyst for developing personal ICT competence as they will use the technology to access the world of information that is available to them beyond the keyboard. As Angela McFarlane (1997) has already identified, the use of e-mail is a quick, cheap and instant way of contacting others (assuming of course that they have e-mail themselves) which invariably provokes a quick response. It is amazing how often people respond quickly to an e-mail but not a telephone message. It is also remarkably cheap as messages can be composed off-line and sent anywhere in the world on completion in a fraction of the time that a corresponding telephone call would take and at a fraction of the cost. E-mail also provides a kind of anonymity for users to ask questions that they might otherwise be too reticent to ask. Although the user's name may be present, there may be little clue as to their age, gender, nationality or even where they have sent the message from. An e-mail from the room next door looks identical to one sent from the other side of the world. Although this relative anonymity may preclude the respondent from replying, it also gives the sender a certain degree of cover if that is what is required! The use of e-mail has also spawned an etiquette and features all of its own, such as user or news groups for those who have specific interests and who can engage in like-minded discussion on-line. By using Internet Relay Chat (IRC) this can be conducted in real time, a cheap and classroom-available means of instant communication with anybody anywhere in the world. However, safeguards need to be taken to ensure that children are not subjected to unsuitable discussions.

As far as the children in our primary schools are concerned, the document *Information Technology: A Scheme of Work for Key Stages 1 and 2* which the DfEE and the QCA jointly published in July 1998 unsurprisingly makes specific reference to the place of e-mail in the primary school curriculum. In a very detailed but realistic unit 3E, the document states that '. . . children learn to use e-mail (electronic mail) to send and receive messages. They learn about communication over distances and will need to consider and compare different methods of communication'. It goes on to say, 'Using e-mail can help children develop their reading and writing skills and develop their knowledge of their wider community. The unit requires collaboration with other schools . . . Children will apply what they have learnt in this unit when using e-mail, gathering information, developing collaborative projects, and writing for other audiences.'

In terms of differentiation, the expectation is that by the end of the unit '*most children will send, receive and reply to e-mails; develop and refine text messages*'. Some children will be able to '*send text and images as attachments*'. Although the document places the introduction of e-mail as a Year 3 activity, it can be seen to be part of an overall strategy of continuity and progression that one would expect from a scheme of work. Year 1 unit 1A talks about *Assembling text*, while Year 2 unit 2A is entitled *Writing stories: communicating information using text*. Unit 3A refers to *Combining text and graphics* and unit 4A extends the idea of e-mail by being about *Writing for different audiences*. Arguably, this might have been better served as a Year 3 activity, as it would then have direct relevance to sending e-mails. Nonetheless, there exists within the document a clear strategy for the development of the use of e-mails across the curriculum. Certainly, children need not and should not wait until Year 3 before embarking on the use of e-mail. Indeed, one criticism of the document is that it tends towards ICT skills rather than ICT application in a subject-based context. There may be very good reasons for using e-mail earlier in a school career – perhaps in a geographical context of communicating with others in a distant locality or contrasting environment.

So where does this leave the pupils in our schools regarding the place of e-mail? What does ICT offer not only the youngsters but also the teachers, lecturers, organizations and companies that are seen as such a crucial part of the NGfL strategy? How and why can ICT fulfil its place as a major means of communication in the new millennium? And, above all, how will children's literacy needs be affected and, as a consequence, be met?

In many ways e-mail should provide teachers with an easy way into using new technologies with children. Schools do not have to be particularly well developed in their use of ICT in order to benefit from what e-mail has to offer. Indeed, it could stimulate a very productive and constructive use of the computer, possibly from a very low starting point. Word processing, or what many teachers perceive as word processing, has been the preferred use of the computer for many years in Britain's schools. Although much pupil use of ICT has often been restricted to using the computer to copy up work in best, this is irrelevant in the context of e-mail. Although it may not be using the full potential of the word processor, it is developing the essential skills that using a keyboard to compose e-mail demands. The immediacy of e-mail will ensure that composition of work away from the keyboard will cease. Even the least confident of teachers should quickly be able to understand the powerful advantages that e-mail has to offer.

As Sue Brindley has already identified in Chapter 1, effective use of word-processing packages with children completely alters the act of writing. The ability to change font style, size or colour to emphasize words, phrases or meaning, to re-order individual words, phrases, sentences or whole passages of text are powerful facilities. Additionally, work can be edited and redrafted without any traces of the many changes that it may have undergone in its evolution and still finish up with a professional appearance that leaves no trace of these changes. To the reluctant writer this may have an emancipatory effect and redrafting will evolve into editing, itself a higher order literacy skill. Whether this is done by the original author or by peers, the emphasis is on changing text to make it better, rather than rewriting it. How many children have been put off this very important stage simply by the fear of having to do too much laborious rewriting? There will be no need to write the whole piece of work out again. These advantages can just as easily be applied to e-mail, either directly in the composition of the message itself or as a piece of work sent as an e-mail attachment.

However, to perceive e-mail as purely on-line word processing does it a grave injustice, even when quite advanced word-processing techniques and skills are involved. The use of e-mail dramatically extends and alters children's written language in two main ways. First, it can rapidly expand the audience that the children write for and secondly it can engage the children in a different type of writing, one that they perhaps haven't had experience of before; that is, the framing of expert questions.

Traditionally, much of children's creative writing has had an audience of one – the class teacher. Primary school teachers have often been in the situation where a creative writing task has been given and the children have gone away with the sole intention of producing something that they know will satisfy teacher. With a little practice some will know exactly what is required in order to fulfil the task with a minimum of effort and maximum positive response from the teacher in return. Although they may share their work with individuals or groups of children within the class the composition of it is essentially a solitary activity. Even where writing tasks are set as collaborative efforts practical organizational issues determine that written work seldom extends beyond the classroom where it originated. The authors may get to read it out to the whole class or even to the whole school in a class assembly and it may be produced in best and displayed on a wall somewhere for parents' evening. As long as it fulfils the designated teaching and learning objectives then ICT will have been seen to have achieved its intended purpose, but the maximum exposure for it will remain within the school.

However, when new technologies are involved there is enormous potential for this audience to be dramatically broadened. Children might compose stories or poems either in a word-processing package or within e-mail and then send them to other schools that are on-line. These might be schools with which they have created special relationships in contrasting environments or distant places and could be anywhere from the school down the road, to one the other side of the county, the country, Europe or the world. Schools where Modern Foreign Languages are taught could set up exchanges with schools, organizations or individuals abroad. If the work is displayed on the school's own website then the audience is potentially anybody in the world who is on-line, and not only schools. The potential audience runs into hundreds of millions of people – many more readers than for most books in print! By including an e-mail button on the Web page, the children could receive responses from anybody who chooses to access and read it. Collaborative writing tasks can be established by children composing work and then sending it either as e-mail or as an e-mail attachment to another school. Children in these schools could then make suggestions as to how the work could be developed – either with creative input, alternative ideas or possibly even continuing the work themselves. This work might then be forwarded to other schools, children, adults and organizations. It is a natural extension of the class task where a child or a group of children each writes a continuation of the work. It might never end! Rather than compose work and share it with children in their own class who act as a critical friend, the critical friend could be in another town, country or continent. Work could be developed at the click of a button, all at the cost of a local phone call. By judicious use of sending e-mails at certain times of the day, time zones could be used to advantage. Children could compose work one day, e-mail it and a child the other side of the globe could read and respond to it. Then the original author could read any changes and suggestions the following day. Niki Davis (Somekh and Davis, 1997) describes an example of how a class acted as an editorial team with a partner school and a school in North America. Two schools produced the first two chapters of a story including the theme of Native Americans but they were presented as a stereotypical view of 'Red Indians'. These were then e-mailed to a school in America for correction and development. The opportunity was taken to alter the stereotypical views and a more suitable ending was included. This kind of explicit use of e-mail to challenge stereotypical views and re-educate or reinforce positive views of multiculturalism can have a significant impact on children.

In many ways the use of e-mail to exchange ideas about the development of work is purely an extension of the collaborative learning tasks in which many schools already engage. This is possibly the most crucial contribution that e-mail can make to the classroom. The notion of children working collaboratively to enhance the experience of learning by the use of new technologies is one that has been explored elsewhere, most notably by Crook (1994).

Unless care is taken in the organization and planning stages the use of a computer by a child can be a very solitary activity. The framework for software evaluation provided by Kemmis, Atkin and Wright (1977) describes four paradigms of software types, starting with the computer controlling the child and progressing through a continuum to the child controlling the computer. However, even if the child is in control of the computer, or using ICT as a tool where the computer is acting purely in 'workhorse' mode, it is important that the user does not become isolated from either peers within the classroom or peers around the world by the solitary use of the computer.

Possibly more challenging are the intentions of the National Grid for Learning to link schools with expert institutions and organizations as mentioned in *Connecting the Learning Society*. Here children will be able to directly e-mail experts in a given field with specific questions related to their school work. Although in the past this was always possible through writing letters or sending faxes, this seldom happened in practice. The fact that many experts have e-mail addresses, often displayed on Web pages, makes them much more accessible than in the past. As a result of this, children now have a direct link to individuals or organizations that are acknowledged experts or authorities in a given field. Quite apart from the fact that this will develop children's own knowledge and understanding of the topics that they are studying it will also ensure that they will have to frame questions to the individuals concerned carefully. Once again, they will have to give due regard to the audience for which they are writing and will out of necessity have to conform to e-mail etiquette. The questions that they ask will have to be framed in a way that will elicit not only a quick response but also one which answers the question that they have posed. If an expert is receiving possibly several hundred questions during a week, he or she will need to be able to read the question quickly and easily, click on the reply button and give the answer to the question.

Many schools are already discovering the power and potential of e-mail as they go on-line. Mayfield Junior School in north-east London (name changed) has been on-line since January 1999. Since then the pupils, parents, governors and former pupils have been communicating to experiment with what e-mail can offer them. As a result there has been a very definite evolution in the way that e-mail has been incorporated into the curriculum.

One of the first e-mails that the school received was from a parent commenting on the school's brand new website:

> An informative guide to the events and work of the school. Would like to see inclusion of SATS results.

This instantly suggests where parental priorities lie! As far as the curriculum is concerned, the children very quickly became involved with e-mail to report back to the school on what they thought about the new website which was starting to make a big impact. Another parent wrote:

I am pleased to see that you are encouraging our children to explore all aspects of computers . . . this website will evolve over time and I look forward to viewing this development.

The parent went on to mention that he had a lot of computing experience and that he was willing to volunteer his services in the future to help maintain the website.

The early e-mails into the school were giving feedback on what the new website looked like. At this stage the communications were very much of the chatty, friendly and complimentary type – possibly low level in terms of 'educational' content but crucially important in terms of establishing e-mail as a forum for discussion about issues involving the school.

It also tempted pupils who had recently transferred to secondary school to make their observations:

I have been on your Web Site and I think it is smashing. On Thursday I had a nose bleed in Frech (sic) and I got it all over my books. So I got to MISS all of my FRENCH LESSON.

The type of children's learning and interaction with each other was subtly changing. How many secondary school pupils traditionally talk to pupils still at primary school? Other discourse followed, this time from one of the governors:

I have just visited the school's web site for the first time and wanted to be one of the first governors to congratulate you on an excellent and informative piece of work. Both of my children were very excited to see some of their work and I am sure they will want to keep visiting the site to see what's new (or as they would say what's 'cool'), we may need a bit of fund raising with our increased phone bill!!!

At this time pupils who were on-line at home started to send e-mails to the school:

Hello! I just E-MAILED to say hello and tell you that your web-site is really good and I've looked at all the things on it! See you on Monday. Bye!!

I am testing the e-mail on our computer it has gone quite well. The school web site was good too. we looked at it on Friday 15th January. My mum would have preferred it if there was a picture of me on it.

I would like to say that I think that the web site is excellent!!! I like the cool pictures and the fab text. I was really excited when I got connected to the Internet and I was even more excited when I saw the web site. I really like it, but I think you could add more information about the staff and more information about Year 5 to improve it.

A previous visitor to the site sent another message about a week later:

I like the changes that have been made to the web-site, it's a great improvement!!! Hopefully there will be more changes made in the future so that it will be even better, if that is possible!!!!

I really enjoyed reading it. It was good fun looking at the pictures. But where was your's and the teachers? Here is a picture of me.

For the first time a pupil enclosed a picture of himself as an e-mail attachment. This demonstrated that the pupils often have access to the new technologies at home before their schools, the very place where they are supposed to be given the skills to participate in society. This particular pupil, a Year 3 child, already had the capability to send a picture as an attachment. How many teachers can do this? Clearly the potential of e-mail extends far beyond what it can offer in terms of literacy. In order to attach the photo the child had to have a degree of network literacy and file management skills. He had to compose the e-mail, find the image file among many other files, attach the latter to the former and then send it.

Another pupil developed this idea further by talking about how he used it at home:

I like the web page very much. I would like my class to put something on the site for other people to see. Could we put our photos on there? I like to use the internet especially for getting game cheats and demos of games. We also write to our family and friends in Iraq.

Then a county adviser found the site and became involved:

I've just been into your website page and was most impressed . . . keep up the good work.

There were several more e-mails of this nature up until the end of January. Once into February, however, when the initial flush of novelty value was over, the type of e-mails started to change.

Here are the prime numbers up to fifty.
1 2 3 5 7 11 13 17 19 23 29 31 37 41 43 47
Question: Tell me the prime number nearest to 1000.

This message posed a question from another source and typified the kind of usage that e-mail in primary schools might consist of. Gradually the type of message became more focused on issues rather than general chat messages:

> Could we please have some more things of year 5 because in our section we have other years. We're not trying to have a moan we still think it's cool.

Opportunities for local history issues also started to develop and become evident about this time, as well as links with an ex pupil who was now a teacher in a local primary school·

> I really enjoyed looking at your site . . . it brought back memories looking at the pics of the hall! If you would like to mail some of the children in my school then let me know.

These samples of e-mails illustrate clearly how the act of writing has been fundamentally changed. The content of the message and the medium become important, often to the detriment of traditionally important elements such as grammar, punctuation and spelling. What e-mail offers these children is the opportunity to provide instant feedback from and conversation with pupils, former pupils, parents and governors as well as to develop links with other schools and interested parties who could be of use to the school. Clarity of ideas has been achieved with punctuation, exclamation marks being extensively used, possibly three times to emphasize a particular point in a chatty, friendly style. This would not happen in many traditional forms of writing as it would be deemed inappropriate. As McFarlane (1997) has pointed out, this 'chat' mode is more akin to everyday speech rather than the traditional form of letter writing. During the Spring Term of 1999 e-mail in society as a whole was still developing and in this school it was very much in its infancy and was offering experiences which were new, novel and largely social. However, as has been seen, as time progressed so did the type of e-mail exchanges between the pupils in the school and the senders of the messages.

As far as the class teacher is concerned, one of the main issues will be managing the use of e-mails in the classroom. As Poole (1998) observed, '. . . managing e-mails can be like trying to steer an avalanche! Harnessing the natural exuberance of children can quickly become a problem, especially when replies start to come back to the classroom. The more letters the children write, the more replies they receive, which leads to a greater demand for computer time.'

Clearly there are going to be many implications with the widespread introduction of e-mail into classrooms. There will need to be a fundamental rethink about key issues such as classroom organization and management, how children learn and what the nature of literacy really is, as well as crucially the number of computers with e-mail access. However, the benefits will inevitably far outweigh the disadvantages.

The book *Connecting Schools, Networking People* published by the British Educational Communications and Technology Agency (BECTa) in 1998 carries a table that summarizes nicely the benefits that use of electronic communications can bring, many of which can be seen in the sample e-mails above. Under the category *Improved motivation and attitudes to learning*, it is stated that e-mail provides a real respondent in an actual context and purpose, as well as encouraging what Moira Monteith (1998) has called 'peer group editing'. This takes place through a review of the main elements of writing such as content, spelling, syntax and punctuation. The next category, *Improved subject and vocational learning*, mentions that use of electronic communication gives first-hand access to local unpublished information, provides personalized answers to pupils' own questions and gives pupils time to work out replies at their own pace. If Internet Relay Chat is used, the learners are actively involved because an immediate response is required. As anyone who has used this knows, this immediacy can be very stressful, as the respondent has to think of something suitable, witty or relevant at very short notice. Indeed, this mode has occasionally been likened to the use of the citizen band radio, which was very popular before it was legalized in the early 1980s. The inclusion by the pupil of his photograph as an e-mail attachment illustrates that opportunities are presented to develop network literacy in the ability to access and transfer files between computers, as well as extending the traditional skills of reading, writing, speaking and listening. Pupils' *independent learning and research skills* will be developed as they pursue their own enquiries by having access to distant experts and native speakers.

So the power of electronic communications is destined to give British schools a powerful tool that they can use easily and effectively. The pupils in our schools have been offered a real world communication system that they will be able to use in a realistic, real world context. Schools will no longer be individual, isolated communities whether they are a few yards or thousands of miles apart. This alone should irrevocably change how children learn – failure to do so will mean that so many important opportunities will have been lost. These are powerful opportunities that must be accepted with alacrity.

REFERENCES

Barker, R. and Franklin, G. (1998) 'Information and Communication Technology – the victim of the Literacy Hour', *Focus on Literacy*, MAPE.

British Educational Communications and Technology Agency (1998) *Connecting Schools, Networking People*, p18, BECTa.

Crook, C. (1994) *Computers and the Collaborative Experience of Learning*, Routledge.

DfEE (1997) *Connecting the Learning Society*, Government Consultation Paper, DfEE.

DfEE (1998a) *Teaching: High Status, High Standards*, Circular Number 4/98, London: HMSO.

DfEE (1998b) *The National Literacy Strategy: Framework for Teaching*, London: DfEE.

DfEE/QCA (1998) *Information Technology: A Scheme of Work for Key Stages 1 and 2*, London: HMSO.

Kemmis, S., Atkin, R. and Wright, E. (1997) 'How do students learn?' working papers in *Computer Assisted Learning*, Paper 5, Centre for Applied Research in Education, University of East Anglia.

McFarlane, A. (1997) *Information Technology and Authentic Learning – Realising the Potential of Computers in the Primary Classroom*, London: Routledge.

MacLeod, H. (1998) presentation of paper to SEDA Conference, University of Southampton.

Monteith, M. (1998) 'Peer group editing and redrafting', *Focus on Literacy pack*, MAPE, p. 5.

Poole, P. (ed.) (1998) *Talking About Information and Communication Technology in Subject Teaching*, Canterbury Christ Church University College.

Somekh, B. and Davis, N. (eds) (1997) *Using Information Technology Effectively in Teaching and Learning: Studies in Pre-service and In-service Teacher Education*, Chapter 13, p. 167, London: Routledge.

Stevenson Report (1997) *Information and Communications Technology in UK Schools: An Independent Inquiry*, London: The Independent Schools Commission.

Chapter 6

Bitesize Learning: An Evaluation of Four History-based CD-ROMs

Becky James

On the day that I sat down to think about this chapter, I ate lunch with a perplexed colleague whose food had gone cold while he quizzed a boy on why he found *Pokémon* so addictive. His answers – along the usual lines of 'It's fun . . . You can play it and save it and collect characters with the cards . . . It's fast and exciting . . . It doesn't take too long . . . Everyone's playing it' were nothing new. Anyone familiar with the Nintendo or Playstation generation of computer games would recognize the comments, albeit with a sigh.

Teachers may grumble over the squabbles these products induce and how children can be distracted from the immediacy of their appeal back to the world of the classroom. Parents can be left out-of-pocket by the breathless pace of media-manipulated fads: from the relatively inexpensive yo-yos of yesteryear to the more obviously lucrative *Pokémon* games and their spin-offs. Mobile phone sales targets have moved downstream from the high point of pre-Christmas sales in the mid-teen market to the primary school consumer: at the dawn of the new millennium, streetwise eleven-year-olds are being targeted as consumers. But any old mobile phone just 'won't do': it has to be one which will relay text messages instantly, play a host of jingles as well as the latest games. Educationalists may react to this phenomenon in much the same way as parents did to the advent of television in the early sixties – with horror and fascination in equal measure. Adults may fall back on television as a cheap option to occupy children's time; they may be left breathless, though, by the quickfire delivery of children's TV presenters or the frenetic pace of 'live' show formats of Saturday-morning television such as *Live and Kicking*. It all amounts to the same thing: a cultural melting pot so fast-moving that 'bright and breezy' are outdated and bursts of Pentium-processor-type energy are of the essence.

Debate rumbles on about the problem of getting young people to concentrate on the printed word when the culture of their world outside school is constantly beckoning them away from the world of the printed book. The same friendship group who had their Gameboy confiscated over lunch, I later noticed engrossed in one of Terry Deary's *Horrible Histories* series 1. Two of these boys – twins in Year 5 – repeatedly opt for this genre of fact-and-fiction text in free reading time. They share, in different measures, a love of the cartoons, the short chapters, the illustrations and the humour: 'Look at this bit on Charlemagne, miss – "Roland and Oliver . . . men behaving sadly". Get it?' But above all, they seem to like the fact that, 'You don't have to read them (the books) from beginning to end . . . one of us can, um, read the first chapter and the other one can be reading the last bit . . . it doesn't really matter about the order, does it?'

Contemporary school-age readers then are encultured more and more into applying short concentration spans to tasks, while teachers need to be increasingly resourceful in developing pupils' skills of reading narratives. Boys in particular, in the past, may have progressed from reading cartoons, such as *Asterix the Gaul*, to an interest in the Romans; currently they may also jump from 'fact'n'fiction' blends, such as the *Horrible Histories*, to research printed resources such as history textbooks. It is surely not coincidental that the large-volume secondary history textbooks of the 1970s and '80s have moved from the thick texts spanning over a century each, to seminar studies divided into chapters on different topics. Ease of delivery and rapid absorption of information has found its way into the 'A' level curriculum too, it seems.

The reason that children argue about mobile phone brands, younger ones swop *Pokémon* cards and 'cheats', while others compete to be the first to read the latest Jacqueline Wilson or J. K. Rowling amounts to one thing; they are motivated to do so. Just as the *Horrible Histories* or the novels of Jacqueline Wilson can be useful stepping-stones to longer chunks of text, so CD-ROMs are key in motivating, challenging and developing skills needed to cope with longer texts in a world of soundbites and quick gratification.

Castle Explorer is an 'edutainment' text combining education and entertainment, fact and fiction 3-D objects, Stephen Biesty's superb illustrations and over 30,000 words of text. Dorling Kindersley market it as 'a mix of history lesson and adventure game, where you explore the 3-D illustrated rooms of a 14th century castle disguised as one of the inhabitants'. This is not a dry, educational text: it combines scrollable and beautifully painted cross-sections of the castle with atmospheric sound effects and text bites. The effect is compelling.

The visual text is paramount and the detailed written text comes to life through the reader interacting with the screen. The reader can view the castle from every angle, zoom in for a closer look or step inside as a real inhabitant would do. The text does not indicate where to find facts as would a contents page in a printed text. Instead, it entices the reader to engage with, be surprised by and unconsciously learn from its linked texts. The home screen gives an aerial view of the castle, framed by ten icons. The reader is set the task of completing the King's mission and exploring the castle as a spy, in the persona of either a maid or a knight. Motivation to learn exists because there is a purpose in finding out information. The task requires the reader/spy to give the answers to four questions, which change each time the story is read, and to find the pieces of a map that will pinpoint the bad Baron Mortimer's escape tunnel. To help in the quest, the reader can access a set of on-line books – the Infopaedia. Other screens include a Word Search with 'hot' text for quick clues and a Spy Chest for hiding useful objects. If confused, the reader can return to the Guided Tour.

Castle Explorer (1996) is what Neate defines as a true information text in that it

> enables the reader to select parts to read and these can . . . be read in any order, or missed out. It has a factual bias . . . its language includes specialised terms . . . which may demand prior knowledge or include unfamiliar concepts . . . The present tense is used . . . headings are used to break down sections to enable the reader to select parts to read . . . glossaries or footnotes are often used. (Neate, 1992, p. 12)

The program design incorporates a number of multimedia features to draw the reader into an imaginary world, full of suspense and uncertainty. Clicking on icons on the Home Screen reveals minute cross-sections, each with its own full screen close-up. Hot spots are indicated where the arrow changes to a hand; clicking demolishes stonework or peels off thatch to reveal scenes below. Sometimes the reader is rewarded with humorous cameos; one such hot spot reveals two people in a 'garderobe', complete with sound effects. Scrolling to one portcullis sparks an invasion; highlighting it activates stereophonic war cries. Other hot spots produce text pop-ups describing weapons in detail, cross-linked to the Library. The reader is enticed to collect gold coins, which are camouflaged in the scenes. (If selected, they disappear from the screen and reappear in the Spy Chest, for use as a bribe later.) Playful moments like these can provide a 'fun' breathing space from the minutiae of the drawings. As I found out when sent to prison, the interactive gaol is a black screen, which dissolves to reveal what initially appears to be a door-hatch through which a gaoler is looking out at the reader. In fact, the gaoler is looking from the outside of the gaol into the cell. He tells me that he can be bribed to unlock the door (if I've collected enough gold coins!). This type of hands-on immediacy engrosses the young reader in much the same way as *Pokémon* does.

The reader-as-spy can enter the 3-D rooms and interact with the inhabitants through live-action film clips; these give a real 'feel' of what it must have been like to have lived in a medieval castle. The reader has to suspend disbelief and actively take on the role of the spy. When investigating the program, I took on the persona of the maid. After knocking twice on the kitchen door, I found myself being told off by an irate cook, demanding to know where I had put the fish I should have collected for supper. My ignorance of this simple task was obvious to the cook, who immediately became suspicious. The cook looked directly at me and demanded answers to questions, framing her words in the second person narrative voice. This increases the atmosphere of realism and tension, drawing the reader into the medieval world. I felt impelled to react immediately and choose one of three options: withdraw from the scene to search for the fish (by using the Search icon), bypass the scene by pressing the Cancel button or ignore both the task and the cook and try to enter the room by clicking on the door again. By a process of trial and error, I found I could access the relevant information by clicking the Key Word list, or ignore the problem and leave it as a gap in my knowledge which might ultimately lead to me being identified as a spy. The reader is manipulated, then, by the text and does not know whether or not that gap is important in the context of their role as spy. Will they be caught out and sent to prison if they skimp this task? By the time they find out, it may be too late!

The sophisticated sequences provide a sense of immediacy because of their high level of interactivity. If the reader does know the answers to puzzles set by the 3-D characters, they can enter their domains: kitchen, solar, armoury and cellars. These views can be scrolled through 360 degrees. Archways can be walked through, cupboards opened, containers moved, curtains tweaked. Children respond enthusiastically to the 3-D characters because they are believable and sometimes frightening and their reading histories tell them that the obvious 'baddies' will ultimately be defeated. By the time the reader has explored the rooms of the castle, they will have been absorbed by the virtual world and will have unconsciously taken in a startling amount of information. If they repeatedly explore the same screen by clicking on its hot spots to discover the different effects this produces, closure, in the finite sense expected in a conventional, word-based text, will not necessarily occur. Resolution can, to borrow from Lewis, 'be postponed, delayed or avoided altogether because the structure of the text is essentially repetitive' (Lewis, 1990, p. 143). However, the young readers I watched using *Castle Explorer* were so absorbed in playing with the surprises available on-screen that they did not seem to mind that they had not gathered all the information necessary, in their role of spy, for a successful invasion of the castle. Having fun was their priority!

Hot spots in *Castle Explorer* can tempt the reader away from completing the quest by encouraging them to pause and explore certain sections of words or pictures. However, the given task of succeeding as a spy provides a hook pulling the reader forwards. The sub-tasks meted out by the 3-D figures are manageable because they are in short units and failing to complete them does not necessarily deny access to other areas. But in diverting the reader's attention away from the cross-sections, the sub-narratives concentrate enjoyment on the video sequences for readers with shorter concentration spans. This CD-ROM is excellent in its capacity to teach audiences of differing ages and abilities about castle life, allowing them to control how much information they access, while encouraging empathy, a learning target in History at all Key Stages. The video sequences invite children to use their imaginations: What would life have been like as a servant? What sort of punishment might spies have received? Would medieval life have been better as a man or as a woman?

Where in Time is Carmen Sandiego? (1998) fuses fiction with non-fiction in a sophisticated design. It borrows the classical theme of a series of quests (in 13 settings from Ancient Egypt to 1960s America) to be solved by combining historical facts with lateral thinking; the reader is the potential conquering hero or quester. The main characters, Carmen Sandiego and her gang, steal a top-secret time travel device (a Chronoskimmer) to go back in time and grab valuable historical loot.

- *Identify the theft!* Talk to the historical characters (by highlighting existing questions, which appear in a rollover bar at the bottom of the screen) and find out what item has been stolen.
- *Solve the problem!* The acts of thievery could change the course of history. The reader must search for clues to discover the particular problem a theft has caused.
- *Collect the Carmen notes!* Carmen has given each of her thieves a note telling them where to hide so she can return to pick them up.
- *Arrest the thief!* If the reader can piece the Carmen note together, the Chronoskimmer will help the reader decode the note and discover where the thief is hiding. They can then activate the Time Cuffs and capture the crook. Children really enjoy this!
- *Acme Good Guides* Within each time period, the reader is helped by a 'Good Guide', each with a particular area of historical knowledge or expertise. By clicking on this guide, a range of ideas is given as to what to do next in any time period, i.e. which area of the screen to explore next.
- *Inventory* In each Case, there are objects the reader can collect. Some characters offer them objects such as tools or gifts. Collectable items can be stored in the Inventory Box at the bottom of the screen.
- *Rollover text* As the reader moves round the screen, the text in the rollover bar at the bottom will change to give helpful information about what they are seeing.
- *Carmen notes* Each note has been torn into several scraps; these appear on-screen one by one, as each part of each mystery is solved; clicking on the scraps will automatically assemble them until the entire note is legible. The scraps are often in the form of a riddle.
- *Acme Chronopedia* This historical guide provides additional information about each period – e.g. important people, maps, events and so on – which can help solve the riddles on the notes. The guide can be 'read', i.e. pages turned, by clicking on page corners. If information from a previous time period is needed, this can be accessed by clicking on the year on the timeline at the bottom of the page. Each setting is equally well documented but a close inspection of just one gives an idea of the raft of skills necessary to fully enjoy it: Case 13 is called 'Shakespeare in Elizabethan England'. A typical conversation between two of the characters (Elizabeth I and the Guide, Renée Santz) starts like this (note the stereotypical gloss on British life – Carmen Sandiego is American in origin):

Renée: England is famous for its poetry and royalty but not for its weather. Let's solve this case before it starts to rain.
Elizabeth: (in a posh voice) I've seen the sun at least twice this week.

If the reader interacts directly with Elizabeth by clicking on her, she points to the Globe Theatre over the river and replies:

Good day, gentlefolk. Just look at that building! By my crown, it has more holes in it than my father, Henry VIII, had crowns!

The rollover text suggests four questions, one of which is 'What have you achieved as Queen?' The text throws up some factual information: 'I've encouraged exploration of the New World and defeated the Spanish Armada. This is truly a Golden Age for England!' As Renée stays silent, clicking on the Queen again prompts her to guide the reader towards the task for this time period:

Welcome again! Just look at that incomplete theatre. It's proved to be a true comedy of errors! That's the Globe Theatre. The actors moved it across the Thames River and are rebuilding it. And I fear their delay may impede tonight's play, to be performed in my honour. William says they're too busy to build. He muttered something about a theft and all the actors having to relearn their lines. Why don't you take my royal boat across the Thames and get my actors back to work?

By obeying this instruction, the reader can click on the 'feet' icon and re-emerge on the far bank, outside the Globe. The Guide draws attention to the fact that sections of the wall are missing and that some scraps of paper are pinned to the edge of the wall openings. These are six rhyming couplets, each taken from a different play by Shakespeare. The task is to enter the Globe, find two more lines of verse which match those pinned to the outside wall and go back and match them up in order to put the wall sections in the right openings.

Clicking on the footsteps fades the screen and the reader is now positioned in front of the Globe's stage, facing Shakespeare and Burbage who are in the middle of rehearsals. Interacting with them makes Shakespeare re-emphasize the problem: scripts are missing and the play must be delayed while the characters learn their lines. Without a script, they need to use lines stuck to the wall as prompts. Couplets from the plays are scattered in front of the stage. Shakespeare instructs the reader, in riddles, to rummage for rhyming couplets from each play and paste them onto a banner: this makes Burbage speak lines of verse aloud. The reader must memorize them and hurry outside the Globe to match the four lines. Only when all sections of the wall are complete may the reader enter the Tiring House. By using the Chronopedia and moving back and forth between this screen and that of the far river bank, talking again to

Elizabeth, it emerges that the Globe was in fact burnt down by a spark from the cannon, a Tiring House prop. Clicking on the cannon makes the Guide fire it and reveal one of Carmen's spies, Medea. The Time Cuffs can be clicked on and dragged across to her; she is then fired from the cannon (the baddies lose again) and the case is complete.

So, genuine historical clues are hidden in each screen and satisfaction comes from detective work, mixed with chases and talking to historical and fictional figures. Each time period can be explored as a separate unit and if the reader doesn't want to tackle all 13 Cases, it doesn't really matter. However, this text cannot be enjoyed to any extent without interaction; the reader must use skills of problem-solving and prediction, deduction, research, skim-reading, decision-making and map-reading. Plenty of hand–eye co-ordination is needed as well as the ability to memorize moves and the effect of hot spots. The reader has to talk to all the characters in each time period and ask them a series of questions – by clicking on them, listening carefully to their comments and then clicking on the further questions which appear as rollover text. The reader must explore the visual text for hot spots, which activate further instructions. Items must be collected and moved round the screen or placed in the Inventory box. The reader must watch for and decode the cryptic Carmen notes, activate the Time Cuffs and research in the Chronopedia before each case can be solved.

Navigating the timeline of the Chronopedia can familiarize children with techniques necessary to use non-fiction CD-ROMs, such as encyclopaedias. Within each period, the reader has to watch for the cursor to change into a feet icon, indicating a hot spot which will take them to another location to collect missing information. Each of Carmen's 'cases' is designed, then, to operate as a discrete historical source of an area of learning. Finding the 'baddie' within each of the thirteen periods in history is the reward. When he or she is caught and punished, historical disaster is averted and closure is achieved.

Titanic: Adventure Out of Time (1996) is from the same genre of interactive multimedia texts as *Castle Explorer* and *Carmen Sandiego* in that it provides video sequences which draw the reader in and uses the reader-as-spy technique, setting the reader tasks to entice them through the text. Information from the multiple sources available appears simultaneously on the screen and sound effects, music, graphics and text screens are synthesized by some slick voice-overs. The reader must employ a range of skills to cope with these, know how to prioritize and access information, as well as assimilate it either for enjoyment or for a purpose such as discovering historical facts or trying to unravel the cause of the disaster. Once again the reader is invited to participate in the drama and follow it through to the inevitable end. *Castle Explorer* uses fictionalized stereotypes of medieval life to mediate the fictional setting to the reader. *Titanic: Adventure Out of Time* offers the reader the role of secret agent aboard the ship, searching for clues and solving puzzles that could alter the course of world history and avert World Wars I and II but this time in a unique facsimile 3-D reconstruction of the doomed *Titanic* and its passengers on its maiden voyage.

The cover blurb of this CD-ROM recalls that of *Castle Explorer*; it boasts 'navigable, fully explorable 3D environments; fluid 360° real-time movement; video sequences from which up to 25 characters address the reader directly, asking questions or giving advice while remembering their movements and acting accordingly'. Some characters give hints or 'cheats' to move the action forward if the reader revisits the same spot too often.

A Guided Tour option again gives an overview. Icons showing cross-sections of the ship enable the reader to access different decks quickly, to walk down or up staircases, through staterooms and corridors, highlighting hot spots as they occur. Exploring these areas at walking pace can be laborious, yet if the pace is speeded up, vital clues can be missed. I was disappointed to find that many bystanders encountered in these walkways seem to move along tramlines with a robotic stare and are not designed to be interactive. Why were they ignoring me? I found myself following them only for them to vanish without having added to my understanding of events. I became disoriented – at one point I found myself in Third Class when I had meant to explore the staterooms. But such fluidity of movement and open access is surely intentional on the part of the software programmers: ironically, I later discovered that many third-class passengers died when the ship sank because they were locked in their cabins, a deliberate policy of the White Star line to keep poorer passengers, who supposedly carried disease, away from the more affluent and powerful. By wandering the labyrinthian depths of the ship I had stumbled on a fragment of knowledge. The different settings of the ship (first-, second- and third-class areas) are painstakingly reproduced, slightly claustrophic and a little too perfect in detail until the fatal collision; again an intentional irony, perhaps.

A different audience might find the sister CD-ROM produced by Europress in the same year – *Titanic: An Interactive Journey* (subtitled *Enquiry into a Disaster*) – more satisfying. More overtly pedagogic than its counterpart, it invites a variety of reading strategies, but visiting and re-visiting different elements of this text are somehow more rewarding. It offers the reader 'intrigue, adventure and the chance to explore the most famous ocean liner in history' but it does not lay on the reader the yoke of averting world wars or changing history! The introduction invites the reader to enquire into 'why Captain Smith continued the voyage despite warnings from other ships'. However, it is a valid learning tool, honing the multiple reading skills necessary when encountering a multimedia text.

The opening screen gives key dates and snapshot photographs of all the navigable sections of the program, set against a watercolour wash of a shimmering, sunlit sea. The background music is calming. As Plowman says '. . . memory and comprehension can be used most productively when the text is clearly structured and navigable' (Plowman, 1995, p.168). *Titanic: An Interactive Journey* can be accessed, enjoyed and understood by casual observers, GCSE students or social historians, albeit at different levels. It will also require and develop different reading skills, providing the user with what

Stannard calls 'a repertoire of experience on which to draw in further readings' (Stannard, 1996, p. 12). The reader may scan the opening screen or open hypertext links to other screens; use the Timeline of chronological dates from 1912 to 1990 as an Index to the diary of events leading up to and following on from the sinking; follow the unfolding drama by clicking on the Tour: a series of atmospheric screens leading up to the disaster, giving the viewpoint of New Yorkers, shipping magnates and families in America only; access technical vocabulary to do with the ship's specifications or read newspaper articles from the first lies fed to the American public – that most of the passengers were safe on board the *Lusitania* – through to the dawning realization of the scope of the tragedy.

The combination of these elements engages the reader's attention in a way that traditional word-based texts cannot and may well engender further research. If the reader simply wishes to be told what happened and who was to blame, without consulting the breadth of sources available in this text and forming their own opinions, then they can take the Tour. If, however, they choose to be shown the tragedy in order to make up their own mind as to the overall cause, they can read more closely, looking at the description of events in more detail through the different media. Taking a particular date as an example, 1912, provides some idea of this. Highlighting 1912 divides the screen in two: the top half presents eight mini-screens, including a photograph of the diving vessel, the *Nautile*, used to investigate the wreck of the *Titanic* and rescue the treasure trove from the ocean floor. The lower screen gives a list of dates, each a hypertext link that can be activated to read a more detailed diary of events. Other hot spots include sepia cameos of crew members, from the lowest rank upwards. Clicking on their faces maximizes them and gives a written profile, which can be clicked on again to be read aloud by a narrator. Passenger profiles are provided but they seem to have been taken almost entirely from the first-class passenger list. Interestingly, accessing the link to the list of survivors at this point illustrates the fact that the aristocracy and influential businessmen and their families were the first ones into the lifeboats, some of which left only half-full. The introduction boasts 'illustrations of first-class passengers, sportsmen and industrial tycoons . . . new video footage of 35,000 metres taken from the *Nautile* sent to explore the wreckage . . . 200 pictures of valuable artefacts recovered from the wreck'. Social commentary in this CD-ROM, then, is more subtle than the lavatorial humour of *Castle Explorer* or the irreverent asides in *Carmen Sandiego* but points up the discrepancies in the official version of events.

The reader can choose to explore the sinking of the *Titanic* by looking at 1912 alone or they can read the CD-ROM as a whole to gain a better sense of the entire succession of events as well as the different agendas of the officials involved including those of the producers of *Titanic: An Interactive Journey*.

Brief encounters with the text may, in turn, point up unanswered questions or produce puzzles which entice the reader into further readings. On my initial reading I had the feeling that the producers had the brief of blaming the ship's captain for the disaster so I decided to read the introduction on the Home Screen again. A second, closer reading provided me with insights I had missed the first time round. Its design, watercolour screens gradually deepening in hue until they overpower the characters within them, worked in tandem with the narration. The first picture showed Ismay, the owner of the White Star line, arriving in London to dine with the shipping magnate who owned the British dockyards where the *Titanic* would eventually be built. The parallel screen is cut away and shows an iceberg field forming in Greenland. The mood of the London dinner-party, conveyed in sophisticated blacks and reds, is matched in intensity by the incandescent greens and turquoises of the icy landscape. The men's conversation turns to a discussion of how the White Star engineers can beat off competition from the German shipping companies to win the prestigious Blue Riband award for the fastest crossing of the Atlantic. The narration builds to a crescendo at the words: 'At the very moment when the idea of the ship is formed, the mountain of ice that will eventually destroy it starts a five-year-long trek towards their meeting-place.' As the screen dissolves to show a large ship under construction, the narrator intones 'They make plans for a gigantic transatlantic liner half as big again as all the others. It is to be a sophisticated floating palace: reliable, safe, pure novelty.' The closing screen of the Introduction shows an iceberg as high as the ship, exquisitely simple in outline and colour, 'a gigantic mountain of majesty moving inexorably onwards'.

This text weaves together diverse threads and viewpoints in the telling of its true tale and the reader can choose whether to pick up one, several or all of these. Different elements of the text; the video footage shot from the *Nautile*, newspaper accounts and recollections of the surviving crew members give a different gloss on events. Each element can be read as a separate unit giving one impression or as part of the whole text giving another. If this Introduction is accessed first, the reader will form different opinions about the tragedy than if they had accessed the information in a different way.

All four CD-ROMs educate and entertain in short bursts of energy. *Titanic: An Interactive Journey* can be read in a random or a chronological order. Accessing information through different media also evokes different responses and different feelings in the reader. *Titanic: Adventure Out of Time* might succeed with a young audience used to a diet of one-player computer games where lone heroes must save vast areas of the planet from impending disaster. *Where in Time is Carmen Sandiego?* romps through history from Ancient Egypt to 1960s America making history accessible to a wide audience while *Castle Explorer* encourages the reader to experience medieval life.

Which brings me back to *Horrible Histories: 'Dark Knights and Dingy Castles'*. At the end of the first chapter, the reader is asked, 'If you were a freezing, starving peasant and you had your glaive at the end of a rich, fat man in a can, what would you do?' That is what history should be about. People. How did they behave? Why did they behave like that? And what would you have done if you had been in their shoes?

Young users of CD-ROMs 'read' in a way which defies one fixed definition because the technology behind interactive texts is constantly evolving. Because hypertext requires the reader to engage with combinations of linked texts, visual and aural literacies are fast becoming as important as word-based literacy. Literacy skills start to mean something different as young people move ahead of adults in learning them. Interactive CD-ROMs engage and inform, surprise and challenge young readers who love the fact that 'it doesn't really matter about the order' of reading: they can choose how to access each element of the text and find the bitesize bursts of information rewarding. Multimedia texts from Gameboy gimcracks, through *Sim-City* simulations to *Titanic* recreations are here to stay. Maybe it's just about time we jumped aboard!

REFERENCES

Printed texts

Lewis, D. (1990) 'The construction of texts: Picture books and the metafictive', *Signal,* **62**, Stroud: The Thimble Press.

Neate, B. (1992) *Finding Out About Finding Out*, London: Hodder and Stoughton.

Plowman, L. (1995) 'What's the story? Narrative and the comprehension of educational interactive media' from the *Eighth European Conference on Cognitive Ergonomics*, September, Granada, Spain.

Sanger, J. (ed.) (1997) *Young Children, Videos and Computer Games*, London: Falmer Press.

Sefton-Green, J. (ed.) *Digital Diversions: Youth Culture in the Age of Multimedia*, London: Taylor and Francis.

Snyder, I. (ed.) (1998) *From Page to Screen: Talking Literacy in the Electronic Age*, London: Routledge.

Stannard, R. (1996) 'Texts, language and digital technologies', *The English and Media Magazine*, **34**, 12.

Multimedia

Broderbund (1998) *Where in Time is Carmen Sandiego?* London: Broderbund Software Ltd.

Dorling Kindersley (1996) *Castle Explorer*, London: Dorling Kindersley Multimedia.

Europress (1996) *Titanic: Adventure Out of Time*, Macclesfield: Europress Software Ltd.

Europress (1996) *Titanic: An Interactive Journey*, Macclesfield: Europress Software Ltd.

Chapter 7

Reader Development in Libraries

Sarah Mears

INTRODUCTION

The way we learn and the way that we find information are undergoing dramatic change. Learning is becoming fluid and continuous, not bound by age or institution. Information and Communication Technology provides the vehicle that makes more information available to help us to make sense of our world and take control of our lives – if only we can access it.

The public library has the opportunity to be at the heart of this profound cultural change. In the first part of this chapter I suggest ten reasons why public libraries will flourish in this new technological world, focusing particularly on the vital services they provide for children. These are that the library is a place:

- for families;
- for the community;
- where many different cultures are recognized and valued;
- for children;
- where computers are used not just for information but for supporting and developing reading;
- for sharing stories;
- for creativity to flourish;
- where children can interact with librarians;
- where individual choice is powerful;
- for learning.

I will go on to describe how libraries are harnessing the power of new technology to reassess and redevelop their fundamental roles – access to information, support for learning and reader development – in new and dynamic ways.

THE LIBRARY IN THE TWENTY-FIRST CENTURY

The library is a place for families, a place where adults and children can teach each other and learn together. Adults and children often find their traditional roles reversing when they are using a computer in the library, as the child will often be showing the adult which button to press next!

A logical extension of this concept is that the library is a place for the community, a place that can provide equality of opportunity, enabling all children and adults, whatever their social or economic background, to have access to Information and Communication Technology. This notion of access is crucial if children are not to be disadvantaged in their literacy development in the future. The power of e-mail, the Internet and everyday applications that will serve as the tools for the next generation of users need to be accessible to all. According to Bob Usherwood, during his Library Association Presidential Address of 22 October 1998, 'The information age will not fulfil its potential if the disadvantaged are excluded or simply fed the popular crumbs from the rich man's cable.'

Furthermore, the library recognizes and values many different cultures and is committed to promoting cultural enrichment. This is evidenced by the growth in non-book based media such as CD-ROMS, video, music CDs and magazines. It is a place where there may be other events, such as exhibitions and reading, drawing in members of the public from a wide range of cultural backgrounds.

A library is a place for children where there are books and other resources specifically selected for them by qualified children's specialists and presented in a child-friendly environment which, unlike school, allows for freedom of exploration. The library is also a place for learning and using information skills, where it is important to locate appropriate information rather than the learning process being led by the technology. Computers in libraries are not used solely for information, they are also an important aspect of reader development on an individual or group basis. For example, children can use them to share book reviews and recommend reads to different people in other locations via the Internet or e-mail. This can be particularly liberating for children who are homebound or living in remote areas.

The library is a place for creativity to flourish. Children enjoy using computers to develop literacy skills. Computers can remove many of the barriers to literacy development thus increasing the motivation to learn. This benefit is further intensified when the place of learning is not associated with compulsion.

A library is also a place where there is interaction with the librarian. Children can develop their confidence in speaking to identified safe adults who can help them navigate their way through the maze of information. The library is a neutral and non-judgemental environment where individual choice is powerful. Children's librarians understand the learning needs of children and can help them find the piece of information that is right for them. The children's librarian is an advocate, guiding book selection without prejudice or judgement of their reading preferences and choices.

ACCESS TO INFORMATION

Libraries have always provided access to the world's information sources. However, the speed and ways of delivering access are changing; libraries have moved from being treasure houses of large collections, to a network of buildings lending materials to each other; to digitized information zipping around the world at the press of a button. Librarians are beginning to act as gate keepers and navigators who can guide learners through the systems to find the information they require and to assess whether it is relevant. For according to Robin Sabin at the Public Libraries Authorities Conference 1998, information overload will be one of the biggest issues of the twenty-first century; librarians' skills will be essential.

Libraries are already at the cutting edge in providing access to information. Facilities currently provided or being introduced include Internet access from public terminals and educational or recreational CD-ROMS to use in the library or take out on loan, all managed by specially designed computerized library management. Some authorities already offer remote access to these via the Internet from school and home. A good library management system can signpost resources, help people identify what medium is right for them, such as a book or video, and give people lots of detail so that they have an indication whether the book is likely to provide the information they want. The management system can group resources by subject as well as by intended audience. Thus, when searching for items on a particular topic, readers can identify whether there is a child's book on the subject which may be more helpful than an adult book for a homework enquiry.

However, in spite of these exciting developments, there remain issues which libraries must address. It is important that the library's commitment to equality is preserved. Children and adults must have equal access to ICT. Adults cannot be allowed to dominate the use of the technology. Preferably the children's library should be equipped with PCs but a compromise could be restricting adult access during core homework times. Furthermore, in the interests of equality, access should be free or, at the very least, a minimum charge levied.

SUPPORT FOR LEARNING

Libraries need appropriately trained staff to help children learn and access information. Whether the information required is book or computer based, librarians need the skills of matching text to readers. Librarians, with a range of media at their fingertips, understand that it is the message not the media that is important. Libraries support formal learning in schools and colleges, adult education centres and distance learning. However, they also support and facilitate informal learning, the learning that begins at birth and continues through life. They support the process of learning to live in society and self-directed learning, whether vocational or recreational, determined by the individual.

Librarians know that learning is lifelong. In a fast moving and ever-changing economy, people need to constantly update their skills and develop new ones. Many people will have more leisure time and will be looking for new interests and ways to expand knowledge and enrich their lives. Libraries can help increase learners' confidence and motivation and help them to acquire good independent learning skills. In libraries learners can set their own pace and their own goals for achievement.

Many library authorities have already set up after-school study support or homework centres working with local schools and the youth service. Homework centres aim to help young people improve their educational attainment, promote learning skills and establish the library as a core community resource for young people by acting as a gateway to information. The centres maximize use of the many resources libraries hold and are the products of partnerships and integrated service planning with other council departments, external agencies and, sometimes, local businesses. Staff in the homework centres provide expert help for children and young people who need support with homework, a quiet place to work and a more informal learning environment. Libraries link with local schools to ensure they know about homework policies. According to the DfEE publication *Extending Opportunity: A national framework for study support* (1998), 'Public Libraries offer an alternative unthreatening environment for young people and provide an ideal place to study.' A teacher quoted in *The Value and Impact of Homework Clubs in Public Libraries* suggested that library-based homework clubs can:

> encourage young people to have a lifelong love of books and learning, give young people the opportunity to learn vital information and research skills, help young people discover the art of serendipity through browsing, and give them a useful first point of contact for community information needs.

Many libraries also offer open learning – mixed packages of ICT materials, books and interactive activities which learners can follow at their own pace and time. These offer support for people at all stages of personal development; from choosing a career, to returning to work, to seeking promotion, to learning life-enriching skills. This includes access to PCs and open learning materials. This is an exciting time for libraries as the role of library staff evolves; they are themselves learning about learning and developing a deeper understanding of the support young people need.

CASE STUDIES

Knowsley opened the first homework club in January 1995 as the library was being resited. The club was run by a children's librarian. Following a successful

European Social Fund bid, they recruited six graduate trainees as 'Study Support Tutors'. Homework clubs operate on weekday nights and during the day at weekends in the larger libraries. Using IT was the crucial factor. Southwark Libraries have eight homework helpers and operate in partnership with Southwark's 'After School Service' in eight homework clubs. The clubs operate twice a week between 4p.m. and closing time. Southwark bought new stock to support the centres in a variety of media – CD-ROM, GCSE study guides and teenage fiction. Plans are also in hand to introduce the Internet. The clubs are reaching a significant number of young people from a wide range of backgrounds and educational abilities.

READER DEVELOPMENT

Reader development means empowering the reader through meeting their needs; giving readers freedom to read what they want, to see a wide range of reading materials, to learn, to be stimulated, to be challenged and to have their potential released. Librarians want people to seek out new reading experiences, new authors and genres. They want to give people confidence and support to be more adventurous with their reading.

Traditionally, children's library services have played an important role in the development of imagination, reading and literature appreciation. Libraries are now beginning to harness the power of the Internet to create an exciting synergy of book and electronic media to enthuse and inspire readers. Technology is not just about information, it is also about imagination. Modern children have a need for literacy skills which go beyond the book. Literacy now comprises many media and libraries need to support and encourage all these literacy skills in a way that is meaningful and relevant.

ICT can do much to encourage reluctant readers. With its interactive potential, its ability to reach geographically dispersed children, its use of multimedia and 24-hour availability, the Internet is an exciting tool to support the development of young readers. Libraries have a role not only in creating their own websites but also in assessing others, signposting sites and actively promoting those which encourage reading and inspire readers.

THE ROLE OF THE INTERNET IN READER DEVELOPMENT

Internet access can promote reader development in a number of ways. By highlighting some of the popular sites that have been positively evaluated by children and librarians I will identify some of the potential benefits that it can bring. Unlike print-based media, Web pages are subject to rapid change. However, my intention here is to highlight issues for general application.

Essex Libraries website (www.essexcc.gov.uk/libraries/)

Essex Libraries, along with many other authorities, have put information about the library service on the Web. An important consideration was to make the website bright, lively and engaging. It was essential that users perceived the library to be relevant and exciting. Children have their own special pages on the site which includes a section called 'Library Fun'. Here children provide their ideas for 'best reads' and have written reviews. There is a review form which children can complete on-line and e-mail to the library service to add to the recommendations. Research by Roehampton Institute's *Young People's Reading at the End of the Century* Project indicated that children prefer to share books with each other than to have them recommended by an adult. A principle of the website design is to provide this opportunity. While books continue to have a central place in the development of young readers' imaginations, websites can complement this by developing and enhancing the reading experience.

Treasure Island's website (www.ukoln.ac.uk/services/treasure/)

This is a pilot project developed by the United Kingdom Office for Public Library Networking to examine how books can be energized by activities around them on the Web. This site gives the visitor background information about the book *Treasure Island*; the author, the characters and tropical islands with links to ships and pirates. There are activities and on-line access to the whole book. Evaluation of this site shows that it has been visited steadily over the two years it has been available and book reviews are regularly received.

The creators carried out research with two primary schools in Birmingham to discover how children used the site. Their studies confirmed that children enjoyed visiting it and had been inspired to read the book. Other key issues identified by the evaluation focused on children's ICT expectations. They specifically wanted more interactivity and sound in the site and the creators felt that they could productively learn from CD-ROM design. If a site is to interest children, it must challenge them and stimulate all of their literacy skills. Internet design and technology is changing daily and children will soon tire of websites that appear dated and dull in comparison to others. An obvious implication is the need for designers to revise and update sites on a regular basis.

An extension of this site, funded by the British Library, with the participation of Birmingham, Bristol and Leeds Libraries aims to investigate how library services can use the Internet to stimulate the imagination of 8- to 11-year-olds. It encourages them to creatively enjoy stories using the Internet and aims to stimulate the development of children's traditional and electronic literacy. At the heart of the project there is a website with pages based around existing short stories and pieces of children's literature. Children are encouraged to contribute reviews and comments about stories to the site and respond to other children's comments. They are also given the opportunity to create their own Web pages. Children are able to e-mail publishers and authors to give their opinions of new publishing projects. There are Stories from the Web clubs in Birmingham,

Bristol and Leeds Library Services where children are able to develop their ICT literacy skills alongside their friends. They are encouraged to complete their own learning logs each week detailing what they have learned, which provides a very detailed and personalized view of the project. A successful bid to the Department of Culture, Media and Sport's Wolfson Fund for Reader Development in Public Libraries in 2000 has enabled nine other library authorities to become involved in the project.

Writers on line (www.yearofreading.org.uk)
The National Year of Reading website provides excerpts from books by well-known children's and teenage authors and gives writing ideas. It asks young readers to think of similar stories and e-mail them to writers on line. They will then receive feedback from 'someone famous' and will see their own work on-line. It also provides in-depth information about particular authors.

The Fiction Café (www.nlbuk.org/fiction-cafe/)
The Fiction Café is the work of the National Library for the Blind in collaboration with the Opening the Book organization and staff and pupils from three schools. Funded by the DfEE, it was developed to promote the books in Braille for teenagers held by the National Library. There are very few places where visually impaired people can go to choose books so the choice has to be made at a distance with very little information about the books available. The readers' opinion survey carried out by the National Library for the Blind in early 1998 revealed that, like everyone else, visually impaired readers want to browse and choose books for themselves.

 The Fiction Café website gives teenagers the opportunity to browse and choose books independently. It has been divided up like a menu, listing special flavours, dish of the day, self-service, main course, etc. Each part of the menu lists some recommended books and members of the National Library can order them on-line. The recommendations are amusing and written in an informal and lively style. There is also a coffee break discussion area where teenagers can discuss books on-line. Readers can contribute reviews using the flavour rating system which runs from 'sweet' to 'vomit'! This site provides a wonderful opportunity for sighted and visually impaired teenagers to contact each other and talk about a mutual interest on an equal footing.

CONCLUSION

Public libraries are at the start of a new journey. It is a journey that needs to be undertaken very quickly and the learning curve is steep. The expectations of their users are growing and the libraries must rise to the challenge. At the heart of the challenge are the young – young readers, young learners and information seekers. Young people still have needs which are best met by traditional library services but equally they need to be exposed to new opportunities for learning.

Libraries will be seen as relevant and exciting when old and new ways of delivering service are seamlessly meshed. The library that is emerging into the twenty-first century will remain a vital community resource and a place for children and young people to learn, to grow and to be enriched.

REFERENCES

Brazier, H. and Jennings, S. (1999) 'How not to make a meal of it: the Fiction Café', *Library Association Record Library Technology Supplement* **4**(1): 10–11.

Children's Literature Research Centre (1996) *Young People's Reading at the End of the Century*, Roehampton Institute.

Denham, D., Nankivell, C., Elkin, J. and Ashley, K. (1997) *Children and IT in Public Libraries*, British Library Research and Development Report, British Library.

DfEE (1998) *Extending Opportunity: A national framework for study support*, London: HMSO.

Library and Information Commission (1997) *New Library: The People's Network*, Library and Information Commission.

Library and Information Commission (1998) *Building the New Library Network*, Library and Information Commission.

Ormes, S. (1998) 'The use and importance of the Internet in literature based services in children's libraries', *The Electronic Library* **16**(6): 379–85.

Raven, D. (1998) 'Report on the 1998 Public Libraries Authorities Conference', *Library Association Record* **100**(11): 594.

Riel, R. and Fowler, O. (1996) *Opening the Book*, Bradford Libraries.

Train, B., Nankivell, C., Shoolbred, M. and Denham, D. (2000) *The Value and Impact of Homework Clubs in Public Libraries*, Library and Information Commission Research Report 32, Library and Information Commission.

Usherwood, R. (1998) 'Knocking at freedom's door: Library Association Presidential Address', *Library Association Record* **100**(12): 638–43.

Part Three
PROFESSIONAL ISSUES

Chapter 8

E-mail: The New Way to Write a Phone Call –
Perspectives of an ICT Novice

Marilyn Foreman

Standing on a mainline railway station, I passed the time by reading most of the print that surrounded me and, in doing so, was confronted by a thought-provoking advert for a multinational telephone company: *E-mail: the new way to write a phone call*. After initially responding with a smile of admiration for the cleverly constructed text, my thoughts, influenced by over twenty years' teaching experience in primary schools, proceeded to focus on its implications for teachers and classrooms. I continued my journey more acutely aware of the speed with which technological change is reshaping and redefining our use of language for learning. According to Topping (1997), in McClelland, 'electronic literacy is not just an additional component to our existing definition of "literacy", it has the potential to transform the whole definition'.

Over the next few years, teachers will be faced with more monumental changes to the primary curriculum as the vision of the National Grid for Learning is translated into classroom practice. Initially only a few will have mastery over the machines they will be using. Learning environments, which to date have acknowledged but not necessarily embraced the opportunities that computers and other equipment have had the potential to offer, are going to be catapulted into the third millennium in a way which will only challenge and interrogate the pedagogy that propels them. Teachers with all subject specialisms will be using a resource of which they themselves may have little experience and technological understanding. It is quite probable that their knowledge of ICT may be less developed than that of their students. What, therefore, are the implications of new technologies and their accompanying new literacies for the non-ICT specialist teacher?

During the last 30 years, the introduction of various electronic machines into the classroom has been largely welcomed by teachers regardless of a possible lack of technological knowledge governing their use. The wider world has become a reality to children through the medium of television to support, for example, the study of geography and science. Tape recorders have provided opportunities for teachers to analyse and evaluate children's oracy skills and have completely transformed our understanding of the way in which children develop as learners and acquire spoken language. Video taping has enabled teachers to reflect on and evaluate their own teaching methods and practices and overhead projectors have broadened the range of methods of delivery in all subjects. Teachers have always felt confident with these conventional classroom machines which are considered to greatly enhance existing teaching practice.

The advent of the computer, though, is presenting a different challenge to teachers. The technologies illustrated above have essentially served to support existing practices in classrooms. The computer, however, is forcing us, as specialists in a wide variety of curriculum subjects, to begin to learn all over again as alongside our pupils we begin to develop new knowledge, concepts and skills within an area of learning over which we have previously felt to have existing expertise. As a result, we are being forced to acknowledge our own limitations within a field of learning with which, to date, we have felt extremely comfortable and confident. ICT does not exist alone as a subject divorced from the rest of the curriculum. It pervades all aspects of life and learning and, therefore, has application across all areas of schooling.

For a variety of reasons, a child's early experiences of school can be at odds with those of their home. At the beginning of this new millennium many children are immersed in an electronically produced culture that is at variance with that of both their parents and their teachers, as Information and Communication Technology develops at a rate over which we have little control. When children read and write using conventional sources and tools they invariably do so alongside an adult who has mastery over both skills. In their use of computers they may well be exercising skills that only one or possibly neither parent, nor their teacher possesses. In relation to 'electronic literacy', gaps between children's expectations and competencies and those of their teachers are considerable and varied. Teachers need to recognize that on entry to school children may have experience of keyboards and screens, fine control of a mouse, have shared and observed the writing process with family members through word processors, e-mail and the Internet and be able to read electronic print. The initial sight vocabulary of such a child may be vastly different from that which is conventionally assessed on entry to school.

I recently read a story composed collaboratively by two six-year-old boys and scribed by an adult in a shared writing context. It read thus:

Once upon a time there was a little rabbit. The rabbit met a bear. The bear was afraid of the rabbit and the bear ran away home. Then, when the bear was running home he met a squirrel. The squirrel said 'Hi!' and he ran off to his friend fox. When the bear saw the fox he said, 'Everyone is scaring me'. Then the hedgehog came up and said, 'Why is everyone scaring you?' Then they ran home. They decided to pick some berries and have a war against some of the animals they met. Then they got a catapult and fired the berries at the animals. They went so fast that they hit each other in the middle and squashed the berries together. Then they got some big rocks and catapulted them at the animals. They shot honey at the bears. Bees came and stung them. The bear and the fox said, 'OK, you've won!' and they never came to the forest ever again. They went back to their own forest and played with their toys – rocks for marbles. Their father said they should not fight and they went back to say sorry. Then they went on their computer and got onto the Internet and talked with the animals – all sorts of things.

In the creation of this story, the boys are making sense and gaining control of their own experiences of life and the power relationships that occur within them. Strikingly evident are the influences of traditional tales which they have heard and possibly read for themselves. The scene of little rabbit, perhaps echoing the tales of *Little Bear*, is reminiscent of the countless tales of animals, like *Chicken Licken*, making journeys through the woods and forests and encountering repetitive meetings with other animals. The emotion of fear is quite naturally explored and they introduce a novel twist at the outset which challenges the generally held assumptions regarding issues of power by having the bear run away from the rabbit and making friends with the other animals. Their knowledge of fables, possibly Aesop's, manifests itself in the concluding moral or message outlined in the final paragraph illustrating their own family codes of conduct.

The story is full of action with very little description. The latter part displays a preoccupation with fighting and war expressed through visual images of cartoon and video game experiences. The boys are well aware of the difference between fantasy and real life and draw the reader into the world of the latter in taking the bear back into the world of his 'own forest' where the 'rocks' are really 'marbles'. It is in this real world that the computer and the Internet exist. These children are bringing with them to school an understanding of adult literacy practices which is undergoing revolutionary change. The Internet is part of their world through both physical and linguistic experience. They become skilled in technical competencies on the computer while developing their thinking, which is both inevitably and inextricably interwoven within it, and enriching their language and literacy development.

Most teachers in primary schools are not ICT specialists and are confronted with the reality that many children may be capable of operating and working with machinery at a higher level than themselves. Our understanding of the scaffolding process, which underpins current educational theory and practice, inevitably prompts us to conclude that we have a responsibility as teachers, with the support of our employers, to involve ourselves in improving our own knowledge of this new technology and the new literacies which emanate from its use. Daunting though it may seem, probably the most effective learning emanates from the teacher being only a few levels above that of the learner. We have all experienced difficult learning situations where our teachers have been so advanced in their subject knowledge that they are unable to communicate ideas at the level that the learner can understand. Similarly, my own experiences lead me to deduce that some of the most effective mentors of initial teacher trainees and newly qualified teachers are those of approximately two to three years' teaching experience themselves who have moved somewhat further along the learning continuum yet can still empathize with and assess the needs of the novice.

It concerns me that in my role as a university supervisor and English lecturer mentoring students experiencing school practice, I have rarely seen computers in use in classrooms. On the few occasions that I have, it has been for the purpose of teaching specific ICT skills and not as an integrated use across curriculum subjects. As a non-ICT specialist who has worked with computers in mainstream classrooms and as part of special educational needs support programmes for ten years and whose, according to Heath (1983), 'learner research' observations of this invaluable tool for the support and extension of learning have been supported by almost two decades of research, I was surprised to encounter environments which did not reflect similar values.

From my own observation of infant children working at computers, I have concluded that one of the most valuable aspects of its use is related to the writing process. Software packages are now available which support children in all stages of writing from planning through to publishing the final version and, as such, word processors should no longer be perceived as electronic typewriters. The self-esteem and written work of many pupils has been greatly enhanced as the word processor has served to eliminate many difficulties that transcriptional aspects of writing pose to some children. The computer has often become the centre for a collaborative learning activity in the classroom due to reasons of access and availability. It has, therefore, proven to be effective as a learning tool, albeit unintentionally, as it has provided the means through which children can construct texts collaboratively. In addition, computers have a highly motivating effect on children's willingness to engage in written activity and therefore greatly influence the attitudes that children bring to the writing task. As a third party to the learning process in the classroom, the computer also provides children with contexts through which they are able to make decisions and solve problems alongside their peers and, in the future, by communicating with other children and adults from a distance. As a result, many higher-order thinking skills are encouraged.

I would suggest three possible reasons that explain why computers are being utilized less frequently than is desirable for pupils: first, it may be that computers have been used unsuccessfully and teachers have lost interest. However, from my own experience as a co-ordinator of Music, Science and English in an infant school, who has explored the potential of computer technology in each of these areas, I doubt if this is the case. Second, they have been bought and never used due to a lack of commitment to the development of new technologies. This may be the case in some instances, where perhaps staff development has not been focused on ICT, but I do not think it would account for such widespread underuse. Third, the arrival of the Literacy Hour has inhibited their use. Chris Johnston (1999) highlights, in his article 'When words are not enough', published in the *TES Online*, 'Teachers struggling with the literacy hour often think of computers as an extra burden.'

The Office of Standards in Education stated that in 1998 inspectors found little evidence of ICT being used in schools that were piloting the National Literacy Project and, furthermore, the introduction of the National Literacy Strategy and now the National Numeracy Strategy is having a vast impact on the management of the curriculum as a whole. So my third reason is possibly feasible. Few references to ICT are present in the framework of objectives of the NLP, a fact which may have impeded rather than encouraged its use.

It would be very easy to supplement the National Literacy Strategy with further reference points to ICT and produce more additional support materials. However, this would be to miss the fundamental implications of teaching and learning in a post-Vygotskian era. As our understanding of the zone of proximal development has been enlarged through recognition of its socio-cultural base so we can begin to examine the value of collaborative learning through a variety of mediating resources, including the computer. Almost all National Literacy Strategy objectives (excluding handwriting) can be investigated and explored by both teachers and pupils using a computer: to identify the use of the computer within specific objectives fails to recognize its full potential as an active contributor to our development as learners. As teachers undergo the training which will greatly enhance their own ICT skills and expertise they will be more able to incorporate ICT into their teaching as they 'model, explain and demonstrate' ideas while at the same time offering its networking potential as a resource for 'questioning, initiating, exploring, investigating, listening and responding, and discussing' ideas (DfEE, 1997). Underpinning the National Literacy Strategy is a Vygotskian approach to teaching which has been under-valued in the prescriptive and often narrowly defined methods of its presentation to teachers and consequently in the implementation of the Literacy Hour.

A rereading of the National Literacy Strategy framework needs to take place; one that moves attention away from the polarized arguments surrounding its content. In reading the objectives, focusing on the verbs instead of the nouns allows for a different reading of the framework, one which uncovers a shift in emphasis away from the National Curriculum for English where verbs tend to be passive in form towards those which are strong and active and which demand and challenge both teachers and children. There are over 100 verbs embedded in the learning objectives, the nature of which characterize it as a curriculum which expects and demands a most comprehensive range of thinking. A Vygotskian interpretation of teaching and learning is implied in the language of its verbs. Thought and language are integrally linked as children learn through socio-cultural means to discriminate, generate ideas, represent, predict, substitute, assemble, classify, evaluate, consider credibility, examine, be critical, design, analyse, anticipate events, empathize, change point of view, transform, parody and invent. A teacher's understanding of the scaffolding metaphor will create the conditions in which literacy and oracy will flourish in their classroom. Over time it will enable the teacher to determine how computers will support, enrich and extend their pupils' learning and help them to discriminate what types of thinking it encourages.

The importance of instruction, essential to a Vygotskian model of classroom practice, is explicitly expressed in the National Literacy Strategy through its emphasis on the teacher being responsible for creating contexts for 'high quality' discourse and 'interactive' learning. The role that computers can play in this process, however, is not subsequently embedded in the framework of objectives. As new technologies act as mediators in such interaction, classroom discourses will continue to be redefined.

It is possible that some teachers have not, as yet, fully exploited the use of computers in their classrooms for similar reasons as those offered by Jones and Fortescue (1987) over a decade ago. They argued that teachers have three fundamental fears: they worry about the complexity of the machines themselves; they may see the computer as a rival; or they may hold a general scepticism about the computer's potential in language learning. At that time these factors probably would have inhibited my use of the computer. One of the most relevant aspects of my own interest in this field stems from the fact that I am far from being an expert in the technology of the machinery itself but have always been happy to be guided by IT co-ordinators, advisers and children themselves. When serious attempts are made to develop classrooms as communities of enquiry and teachers are encouraged to develop as 'learner researchers', it is communally recognized that no one person is the source of all knowledge. Children become empowered, as learners, when they come to understand that their own learning pathway is as highly valued as that of any other person, including adults.

While I was writing this chapter my daughter, who is far more adept at using computers than me, directed me in extracting a word count for a piece of writing. On completion, I asked her to reflect on how she had learnt this function, taking into account that she had received little instruction in using the computer either at home or at school. She replied by describing an investigative approach to learning, explaining that one afternoon when she was younger she had played at the computer with a friend exploring pathways which the *File* menu allowed her to access. Having, therefore, found *Summary Information* through systematic enquiry, on another occasion, after completing coursework herself, she filled in the *Summary Information* table in order to save the relevant data. At which point, she raised her own question 'What does statistics refer to?' Predicting that this would be numerical in context, she opened up *Statistics* and was able to access information regarding her written text including *date*, *editing*, *time* and *word count*. With no adult present the interactive nature of the program and her dialogue with her friend combined to stimulate her reasoning in order to solve the problem for herself and, in doing so, advance her knowledge and skills beyond those of the adults around her. She was not acting as an inferior in learning, subservient to an adult's body of knowledge from which she felt alienated. She possessed the confidence to discover for herself, and the computer, as a resource and tool, had the capacity to facilitate this learning.

The arrival of Internet facilities in schools will inevitably challenge the concept that language and learning development is an isolated process which involves individual extension of thinking. As teachers monitor pupil discourse using new technologies a review of teacher intervention will be called for. Similarly, teachers' own acknowledgement that they are novices in a new field of learning will result in the need for greater dialogue between teachers and their colleagues. The concept of team teaching will be redefined as teacher specialists in a variety of disciplines collaborate to construct new meanings.

We need, as teachers, to broaden our concept of the 'scaffolding' process and to expand it beyond the importance of the teacher's questioning skills. Interactive learning can take many forms and a crucial factor in children's empowerment is the teacher's ability to relinquish the role of key questioner in order to share this role with children on an equal basis. The introduction of e-mail and the Internet in primary classrooms can therefore be seen as a powerful resource for learning for both teacher and child alike. Fundamental to this is the need for similar supportive learning among teachers as colleagues and crucial questions need to be addressed regarding appropriate provision for staff development and human resource management. It is going to be relatively easy to organize strategies to train teachers to operate hardware, to raise awareness of the range of programs available, to provide evidence of children's learning that will persuade teachers to view the computer as an aid rather than a rival and to recognize possibilities of integrating ICT across the curriculum. However, ultimately the success of formally introducing new technologies into classrooms will depend on the teacher thinking inventively when planning for a program's use. National initiatives of recent years have done little to advance creative aspects of thinking among teachers and children and without guidance as to how we use technologies creatively, imaginatively and critically computers will remain purely functional machines at the side of the classroom used only when the need arises. Learning through nationally funded initiatives needs to focus away from the computer as a machine and on to the thinker who is operating it. According to Margaret Meek (1991) 'As a literacy tool, a computer depends on who is in charge'. Teachers will only acquire and effectively use the concepts, skills and knowledge needed to manage classrooms in this new technological age if their own learning is rooted in real-life, socially situated, interactive learning contexts.

As classrooms adapt to new technologies, teachers will need to respond to a new range of difficulties which arise as 'new literacies create new illiterates' (Meek, *op. cit.*). Who will these children be? How will we identify them? How will we address their needs? With regard to conventional print-based literacy, the computer for many children has become an invaluable tool for learning. Working in small groups children have found a constructive means through which they can create texts collaboratively; in doing so they are often able to produce work of a higher standard than is expected when using pencil and paper methods. Children who find transcriptional elements of writing difficult are able to write confidently on the computer in the knowledge that their work will appear equal to that of others when printed. Use of the computer has proven to be a highly motivating channel through which children willingly engage in the writing process. Children have been relieved of the experience that promotes the writing of text as being 'so laborious that the first draft is the final copy, and the skill of re-reading with a critical eye is never acquired' (Papert, in Jones and Fortescue, 1987).

The help that a computer can provide for those with learning difficulties is demonstrated by Mary. Mary was seven years old with strikingly auburn hair and considered 'overweight' by the health conscious mothers of children with whom she attended school. She was shy to the point of silence in school and hated being the centre of attention. She would physically recoil when asked a question, her face would redden and she would hide behind her hair or hope that a friend would divert attention from her. Her movements were particularly unco-ordinated. Her writing was illegible and for two years she had willingly and painstakingly practised her letter formation under the scrutiny of a support teacher in the anticipation that this would improve her control of a pencil. On close observation, it was noted that Mary's strength was in learning Science and her individual educational targets were changed in order to capitalize on her strengths while employing different strategies to influence her progress in writing. She was given the opportunity to work collaboratively in Science so that she could impart her enthusiasm and knowledge of the subject to her peers. Electricity was the current area of research in the classroom and she was able to develop her fine motor skills by constructing simple electric circuits using a variety of tools and materials. Developing skipping to music was the main PE activity that term and the support assistant gave her individual tuition by breaking down movements into short, manageable, multisensory steps which were achievable. In addition she was given access to a computer to enable her to work collaboratively with both adults and other children when she had to perform a written task. Within a very short time the whole appearance of the child changed. A confident girl entered the classroom each morning, she began to ask and answer questions without prompting and her handwriting improved by leaps and bounds although she seldom held a pencil. For the first time she managed to form letters correctly, to judge spacing between letters, to differentiate between size of letters and, as a consequence, to write with enthusiasm and pride. Everything fell into place at the same time. Surely this puts into question linear approaches to learning that current national initiatives expound. There are numerous examples of how the inclusion of computers as a tool for learning has helped children to become literate, especially children who do not perceive themselves to be skilled readers and writers.

While supporting conventional literacies, new technologies also initiate new literacies. One of the overriding responsibilities of training programmes is the need to address teachers' lack of knowledge with regard to the new literacies and this will involve collaboration and co-operation between ICT and English subject specialists. Text on screen is organized differently to text on paper and inevitably requires a whole new range of skills. As with books learners need to understand more than just how to operate with a given resource. The structure, organization, surface and stylistic features of electronic text need to be explored in the same way as written text. All teachers have an understanding of print-based texts, either implicitly or explicitly, but 'very few have experienced the whole range of possible uses for ICT, let alone written computer programs' (Tweddle, 1993). New technologies and the exploration of new literacies need to be an integral part of each other and not perceived as parallel systems. 'Computers provide a new medium (or, more accurately, a range of new media) for communication and therefore imply new forms of literacy. They also provide new contexts in which communication of all kinds is used' (Wray, 1994). Teachers will need to have expertise in both new and conventional literacies, understanding where they interact, stand alone or complement each other.

'What counts as being literate changes in every generation . . . is re-made and re-conceptualised in new settings' (Meek, 1991). The presence of the computer has created that new setting in primary classrooms and will continue to challenge present understandings in the future. It is crucial that teachers adopt new technologies, not as individual tools separate from classroom contexts but integrated within them. They are part of 'an existing culture interacting with many other factors in the social contexts of classrooms' (Wray, 1994), the contexts of which teachers of all subject specialisms have in-depth knowledge and understanding. In the short term many teachers and pupils will be learning to use a new tool and therefore the 'quality of language is likely to be more context specific' (Wray, 1994) but, in time, teachers and learners will enjoy the power and take advantage of the choices that being literate in the twenty-first century brings.

The opportunity to *write a phone call* or receive one through electronic text is an expansion or extension of conventional literacy, not a replacement for it. New literacies and new technologies will enable us to learn more about language and learning and will therefore be fundamental to future teaching and learning contexts. 'Excitement comes from the knowledge that ICT is much more about learning than about technology itself' (Moore and Tweddle, 1992).

REFERENCES

Brice Heath, S. (1983) *Ways with Words*, Cambridge: Cambridge University Press.

DfEE (1998) *The National Literacy Strategy*, London: DfEE.

Johnston, C. (1999) 'When words are not enough', in *TES Online*.

Jones, C. and Fortescue, S. (1987) *Using Computers in the Language Classroom*, London: Longman.

Meek, M. (1991) *On Being Literate*, London: The Bodley Head.

Moore, P. and Tweddle, S. (1992) *The Integrated Classroom: Language, Learning and IT*, London: Hodder and Stoughton.

Topping, Keith (1997) 'Electronic literacy', in N. MacLelland (ed.) *Building a Literate Nation: The Strategic Agenda for Literacy over the Next Five Years*, Stoke-on-Trent: Trentham Books.

Tweddle, S. (1993) *Developing English: Approaches to IT*, National Association for Teaching English.

Wray, D. (ed.) (1994) *Literacy and Computers: Insights from Research*, United Kingdom Reading Assocation.

Chapter 9

Special Educational Needs and New Literacies

Angela McGlashon

> There will be more effective and widespread use of Information and
> Communications Technology to support the education of children with
> special educational needs, in both mainstream and special schools. (DfEE,
> 1988)

For a long time I have been concerned with the opportunities for pupils with
special educational needs to access and use the computers in school. Why do so
many schools give the oldest, most outdated computers to the special needs
department? It would seem obvious, because of their learning problems and the
potential of ICT to enable their participation and promote progress, that they
should be given access to the most up-to-date machines and the latest
technology. In this chapter I outline ways in which using ICT can 'add value' to
children's learning when they have special needs whether they are sensory,
physical, behavioural or learning.

Older computers, such as the BBC microcomputers and the Acorn series, had
many good programs written for them and it was relatively straightforward to
attach a concept keyboard to them. Today's children, and those who will follow,
have a sophisticated idea of what a computer can offer. It does nothing for a
child's self-esteem to have to sit down in front of a program which is slow, very
basic and lacking in pace and interest. Children are often aware that the machine
they are using has been replaced in other classes by more modern and
sophisticated ones. The motivational aspects of using up-to-date computers and
software can be so useful for children with learning difficulties as well as an
excellent use of ICT, which will maximize the potential of the child and the uses
of this great learning tool.

Children with a variety of problems can use the computer to give them access
to information and presentation which is otherwise difficult to achieve. Children
with physical problems can be supplied with switch technology, rollerballs and
touch screens to enable them to activate the programs and on-screen grids to

lessen the number of key strokes needed to operate the program to produce a finished piece of work. In the future head pointers and infra-red technology should lessen the need for too much gross motor movement by making the technology much more sensitive and receptive. Children with motor problems can produce pieces of work with the same presentational standards as other pupils, and can participate equally. This spurs them on to achieve greater degrees of success than would otherwise be possible. It opens horizons for these pupils and demonstrates to them that they can achieve higher standards than they might previously have thought possible. For, according to Richard Ager (1998), 'Children with physical disabilities are going to want to use the computer for the same range of tasks as children of their own age without disabilities'.

Teachers and helpers of these children will also be able to measure their true intellectual ability and treat them in an equitable manner. It has been problematic to make accurate assessments of children with physical disabilities and I foresee that the onset of more access to technologies will enable pupils to successfully demonstrate their capability and teachers to recognize their potential. Nothing encourages children with special needs as much as success, especially when their peer group can see that success is demonstrated on an equal basis without allowances being made.

A key advantage of the use of the computer with children with special needs is the ability for it to model and reinforce skills which pupils have found difficult to acquire. 'Drill and Practice' software promotes overlearning which proves valuable for children with learning difficulties such as dyslexia or speech and language problems. This modelling of skills can be repeated as many times as the student needs in exactly the same way without the pupil becoming bored or frustrated. Multimedia software has the advantage of being able to reinforce this learning in a multisensory way through the use of auditory and visual stimuli. However, children will always need to recognize signs, labels and headlines as well as sign and fill in forms. The sounds, pictures and co-ordination skills needed in programs are important aspects of the way in which children learn, hence the need to have good, multimedia computers for the pupil with special requirements. The school of the future will have in-built facilities for pupils to revisit skills not thoroughly internalized into long-term memory by having databanks, resource areas and computer facilities to enable students to access this reinforcement on demand. In these language resource areas will be talking books and interactive programs alongside reference and games software. All these will complement the standard book corner and give a new dimension to the acquisition of literacy skills.

Some of the most popular software in special schools in recent years has been the integrated learning systems (ILS) which allow pupils to log on at their own level and pace their work to suit themselves. The need for teachers will not diminish as there is still a need for careful monitoring and assessing as the pupil progresses. Furthermore teachers still need to consider how they will use ILS to support creative approaches to teaching and learning. Some of the latest ILS programs incorporate assessment, monitoring and future planning targets which are generated by the computer. The interaction between pupil and teacher that has proved so beneficial in the last few years when setting individual pupil targets should not be discarded. These tutorial sessions can highlight and monitor a range of strategies that are so important when addressing the needs of the individual, not to mention the benefits arising from the co-operation of the child in their own programme of study. According to the DfEE's Code of Practice, 'Children have important and relevant information. Their support is crucial to the effective implementation of any individual education programme. Children have a right to be heard. They should be encouraged to participate in decision-making about provision to meet their special educational needs.'

The potential offered by the computer is not limited to simply providing a means of repetitive drill and practice reinforcement of skills. It can also assist the child with special needs in their creative endeavour allowing them to take control of the computer and their own learning. The need to communicate in written form will still exist in the future although speech activated programs could relieve the burden of composition, and screen readers the burden of reading back. The collaborative aspect of word processing as addressed in many primary schools can further develop and enhance the way in which children can develop their writing skills. Integrated spell checkers, thesauri and predictors will inevitably become more sophisticated and, hopefully, will assume intelligence from the user to accommodate the 'most usual' words and phrases learnt from that person. Grammar checkers will further enhance the ability of all pupils to express themselves in the most lucid way and enable those with learning or expressive language difficulties to express themselves and be readily understood by those receiving their work.

Word banks, subject-specific words and on-screen grids are widely used and, when set up to meet the requirements of individual children, can prove an invaluable aid to accessing the words they need. Not only do these programs encourage a wider use of vocabulary by offering the visual prompt of both the word and the picture or symbol to accompany the word but also the word can be read to them to further reinforce the acquisition of the text. This multisensory reinforcement of vocabulary will facilitate the transference of these words to the long-term memory. In the past these programs have seldom been used for older children or adults. In the future they will prove essential when accessing technical vocabulary or phrases which will be available at one click of the mouse. AutoCorrect is a useful tool that does not seem to be used very often. For pupils with spelling difficulties or for those with motor difficulties, it can provide a bank of codes with which to access frequently used phrases, comment banks or a personalized list of difficult words needed in their compositions.

The reading pen is one of the most exciting recent developments. This enables those with reading difficulties to scan a word via a small hand-held pen scanner and have that word read to them by holding the pen to their ear rather like a phone. These pens also contain dictionaries and memory facilities to enable often-checked words to be revisited or recorded for future teaching sessions. Pens like these could be incorporated into the design of libraries or banks where accurate reading of text is important.

It is not only children with learning difficulties but also children with behavioural problems who find the multisensory approach motivating, non-threatening and non-judgemental in the assessment of their work. A thoughtfully designed program will provide positive feedback and have a fail-safe aspect built in so that pupils will have access to the correct model or result without too many failures which can reinforce the incorrect answer. Pupils who would otherwise find it hard to accept failure or correction from their peers or teachers may accept correction from a computer and might be inspired to try again to achieve a good result. For, according to Hughes (1997), 'One of the best strategies is to involve the child with EBD in positive and rewarding activities. Computers can help create the active and motivating environment in which the learner will experience success.'

Children with behavioural problems may not have the attention span that leads to effortless acquisition of basic skills. There are many excellent basic skills programs that offer incentives to keep trying again in order to progress to the next level. These programs are particularly useful in Maths or English where the acquisition of basic skills can be repetitious. But, couched in an exciting game format, this repetition can be exciting and the resulting success motivating, therefore committing skills to the long-term memory by revisiting and reinforcing. Children with social interaction difficulties often find computers much less confusing than having to deal with human beings. Computers do not have 'grey' areas of interaction. WYSIWYG or 'what you see is what you get' works really well for autistic or Aspergers children who find social situations difficult, confusing or even frightening.

These kinds of applications can also encourage children to discuss strategies with the supporting adult which, in turn, facilitates the assessment process and ultimately informs the planning and provision provided for that pupil. Watching pupils manipulate programs, negotiate through the subject matter, solve problems that occur as well as monitoring their attention span are all powerful ways of assessing progress and application skills. In the future the need to navigate around programs and the ability to recognize common ICT-specific words will prove invaluable. Many programs offer speech support so that pupils can access the information even if their reading skills are impaired, either through sensory difficulties or through specific learning difficulties. This enables the learner to develop independence and encourages perseverance within a task.

Children with visual difficulties can gain access to ICT and the curriculum through the use of enlarged fonts and different coloured backgrounds and screen readers. Most computers have a facility within the basic set-up program by which the visual presentation can be altered to suit the individual. Voice e-mail is already a reality enabling those with reading difficulties to access new communication facilities. There are some excellent screen-magnifying programs which can enlarge and enhance any area of the screen, as well as total-screen readers by use of which information can be scanned into the computer and then read aloud to the recipient. The voice quality of some of these screen readers has been a little robotic in the past but new programs provide opportunities for pupils to choose the gender, pitch and accent of the voice reader. These screen readers also have the facility to read toolbars and drop down menus as well as the main body of the text. Soon most computers will offer the speech support that has been harnessed in educational programs for younger learners in the past and will be extended to more advanced programs for learners of all ages. Slowing down the cursor and enlarging both the trail of the cursor and the cursor itself can prove an invaluable help for those with poor sight. All these things can be achieved through the main control panel of the computer.

Monitors are now produced in a variety of sizes and school whiteboards could soon be replaced with large whiteboard monitors which are touch sensitive and responsive to computer displays. This will help those with visual difficulties and allow them the same kind of interaction as their classmates. The problem with CCTV screens has always been negotiating the way around the page and the inability to see the whole page for reference. By using a huge white screen it would be possible for the reader to see the whole page by turning their head instead of scrolling around the screen.

Keyboarding skills and touch typing have always seemed an obvious help to those with visual difficulties. It is therefore surprising how few students with visual impairment develop their touch-typing skills. The kind of touch-typing program that would help in these cases would have to have voice support and feedback, coupled with a good talking word processor set to read letters or sounds as appropriate. Communication would become increasingly easy with these measures in place especially when using the Internet or e-mail. Speed of touch typing will become increasingly important. Already many young people leaving school have developed this skill which enables them to watch the screen while inputting information via the keyboard. However, modes of input will become increasingly automatic. Touch screens and slide pads will enable much better access to drawing programs and those with basic 'touch and do' type activities. The pen touch screen already dispenses with the need for those with co-ordination problems to develop the mouse drag-and-drop skill that is currently needed in most programs.

Pupils with hearing difficulties require access to written and visual material. Historically there has been a shortage of good signed programs or programs with subtitles. New developments can include soundtracks which, when accessed through a hearing loop or headphones, will enhance the ability of those with moderate hearing loss to participate in a program along with their fellow pupils. Until this becomes commonplace, ensuring that all other background noise is decreased or eliminated can help access to programs for those with hearing difficulties. Many children with mild hearing loss often find it difficult to hear against the background working noise in a classroom. Some children with intermittent hearing loss can have a variety of hearing enhancements which are needed at different times. Headphones are not always the answer as children with hearing aids cannot always use headphones simultaneously. Careful consideration needs to be given to those children with hearing loss and careful monitoring and on-going assessment needs to take place. Word processors that combine pictures or symbols with words can be used for making signs, letters or instructions. Software developers should seize the opportunity to produce more programs that use signing as on-screen captions and symbols. There is a demand for captions for television programmes and the more extensive use of signing support will aid those with hearing loss. Many lively and interesting programs rely on sound and the new literacy could be more strategically developed to accommodate those with hearing difficulties.

Developments in video conferencing could be made available to allow for signed communication between the hearing impaired. The speed at which these images are transferred has proved a difficulty, when the fluency of the image is so important, as a rather jerky image can distort the signed message. Advances in technological capability will produce more fluent images that are easy to read. Video conferencing can further enhance the ability of specialist teachers to teach or tutor sessions without travelling great distances to do so. Perhaps a dual video conferencing system will allow signers to receive images from a conference or lecture and transmit a signed version directly to small screens in front of the recipient. The difficulties surrounding the signer's ability to convey accurately and clearly to all those in need of signed support have sometimes proved to be a problem. The need for clear backgrounds with little visual distraction and the importance of facing the recipient to enable lip-reading to take place can be difficult to accommodate.

It has always been important to give hearing-impaired pupils the opportunity to learn using their strengths and reinforce this learning with as many practical applications as possible. According to Ager,

> Wherever possible children should be participants in practical activities which they can actually be involved in by using their sight. This offers opportunities for using floor robots, analysing the information received from remote sensors or controlling models using some form of programming language. (p. 140)

The advantages of using a computer for children with speech and language difficulties may not seem obvious but there are many creative ways in which ICT can be used to encourage the fluency of language and increase interaction between peers and adults. In fact, if the problem is articulation, it could be that inputting information via a keyboard could form a bridge between physically speaking and contributing to class activities. Communication devices already exist, as do text readers, and future developments look exciting in the field of smaller and more manageable communicators. As the Code of Practice states

> Tl.. school , . . secures access for the child to appropriate information technology, for example word processing facilities, painting programs and software which encourages communications and self expression, so that the child is able to use that technology across the curriculum in school and, wherever appropriate, at home.

Some programs have the facility to record the child's own voice when retelling the story and this enables him or her to sequence and order events as well as recording their voice. This instant feedback gives the child a way to monitor their own progress and measure any successes. Tape recorders and Language Masters can be used to record short pieces of speech and it is fun hearing your own voice being played back to you. Some children are surprised at the sound of their own voices, as we all are to a certain extent, and this gives meaning and clarity to the type of language programme of study being put to them to improve their enunciation with immediate proof of success. Voice-activated programs do not accept a great variety of speech defects or poor enunciation and so, in the future, the ability of these programs to accept a greater variety of registers of tone and lack of oral clarity will prove invaluable to those with articulation problems.

To improve self-expression children can work on a task collaboratively in pairs or small groups at the computer. The difficulty with speech becomes of secondary importance to the need to solve the puzzle or achieve the desired outcome. Limiting the range of vocabulary needed to interact with another pupil enables the child with difficulties to get to grips with the required vocabulary and convey meaning to his peer. Using a floor turtle would involve 'forward', 'back', 'right' and left', as well as a series of numbers to communicate with another pupil to achieve a common goal. There are many programs rich in vocabulary, graphic support and sound effects that would form the basis of vocabulary extension and vocal enunciation practice. The talking book type of program gives children with limited vocabulary the chance to explore other situations for language enrichment as well as being able to model situations or scenarios on their own experience.

Communication is an important element of education and development. Enhancement of communication skills will provide a boost to the acquisition of information and research skills to those with difficulties. Communication is a major thrust of the government's policy to ensure all schools are making the most of the new literacy and technologies. E-mail has enabled those with limited abilities to communicate, ask questions and research alongside their peers. Anyone can e-mail a wide range of institutions, such as government agencies, universities, specialist organizations and personalities for research and communication purposes. The ability for staff supporting those with special educational needs to e-mail means that they will now be able to ask questions and access the most up-to-date research and findings about the difficulty that they are encountering. The mail forums that have been established to support all aspects of special needs have proved immensely popular and the archived subjects that have been discussed have been an invaluable resource to those who have so far discovered them. In the future all staff will be able to access these support groups and facilities and up-to-date information will be e-mailed to them personally.

The ability of future developments in ICT will prove very exciting and liberating to those with special educational needs. Already the wide range of programs and peripherals makes this one of the most exciting aspects of education. It is almost like a great jigsaw; a challenge to find the most suitable aspects of ICT to suit the difficulty and solve it. Every year there are more developments in ICT in special educational needs and an ultimate aim of being able to include a wide variety of pupils with disabilities in our mainstream classes can be achieved by sensitive and careful access to the correct ICT solution to a problem. We can look forward to future developments. According to David Blunkett, writing in *Excellence for all Children* 'The pace of change will be linked to the availability of resources. Action will be carefully phased, bearing in mind everything that is being asked of schools and LEAs. Our objective is . . . sustaining high quality provision for children with special educational needs well into the twenty-first century.'

REFERENCES

Ager, R. (1998) *Information and Communications Technology in Primary Schools: Children or Computers in Control?*, London: David Fulton.

DfEE (1998) *Excellence for all Children with Special Educational Needs*, Green Paper, London: HMSO.

Jeff Hughes in R. Bates (1997) *Special Educational Needs: A Practical Guide to IT and Special Educational Needs*, Oxford: Research Machines.

Chapter 10

Curriculum Development and Implications for the Future

Nick Easingwood and Nikki Gamble

This book has illustrated how the presence of new technologies has redefined what we mean by the term literacy. A range of technological, cultural and social factors has ensured that society has been irrevocably and fundamentally transformed. This, in turn, necessitates the need for an education system that prepares pupils for living and working in this kind of society. The purpose of this chapter is to try to make some suggestions as to what an appropriate curriculum of the future might necessarily look like and how this might be achieved, given the present starting points and existing preconceptions of the latest generation of intending primary school teachers.

Clearly there are implications for the education system as the children in schools will need to be equipped to cope as the first part of the twenty-first century progresses. There will undoubtedly be an exponential increase in the power, scope and capacity of technology over the next few years; the more advanced the technology, the faster the rate of change and as a result of this, the faster society will need to adapt and absorb this change. The need for flexible working patterns and being technologically literate will never be more necessary. Indeed, technological illiteracy could lead to becoming a member of an underclass with a similar status to those who, in previous generations, could not read or write. This means that teachers and the schools in which they work will need to be better prepared to cope with this significant shift of emphasis, which in turn will mean that the institutions which train and prepare these teachers will also need to adapt accordingly. It also raises some fundamental value questions, such as what value do we as a society place on technology in particular and education in general? This leads to some key questions, including what we mean by literacy, ICT and the roles that these play in the current school curriculum and what role they might play in the future. In order to identify and meet the challenges of these changes, we decided to undertake a small-scale research project to ascertain how their students perceived these important aspects of their training and to suggest what a curriculum and a classroom of the future might look like. Before any curriculum development can take place, it is necessary to ascertain what the students think about these aspects of their course, their place in school and society in general. This way, it was felt that there would be a base upon which to build any changes.

However, since the introduction of the National Curriculum in 1989, there seems to have been a range of legislation which has not enhanced but stifled the development of the place of new technologies in schools. It could quite legitimately be argued that while society has moved towards a more flexible mode of living and working, the education system in England and Wales has moved towards a more 'traditional' mode of teaching and learning. The principal danger is that government initiatives such as the National Curriculum and the Literacy and Numeracy Strategies might act as contradictory levers against the requirements of society. At Anglia Polytechnic University's School of Education, we work within the requirements of university regulations and requirements, as well as nationally imposed legislation. In order to fully appreciate the restrictions under which initial teacher training institutions work, it is necessary to set an historical context.

The advent of the initial National Curriculum for pupils in 1989 placed the computer firmly on the agenda as Attainment Target 5 of the Technology document (it took years to separate out Information Technology and Design Technology). This was the first time in English educational history that ten curriculum subjects had the status of being compulsory and the use of the computer was one of them. It also introduced for the first time the schizophrenic nature of Information Technology in the curriculum. All curriculum areas, with the exception of PE, specifically mentioned the role that IT could have in supporting teaching and learning as a resource tool to learning. In contrast, the very existence of a document for IT implied the question of whether IT is a resource to learning or a subject in its own right. However, the IT document, especially the 1995 post-Dearing version, illustrated an approach that was geared towards the application of IT rather than the explicit teaching of IT key skills. The 2000 version of the National Curriculum does little to clarify this situation.

The contention of this book has been that Information and Communications Technology effectively does not exist as a subject; it is a tool to learning and no more. Although taught as discrete subjects in secondary school and also within Anglia Polytechnic University's School of Education under the banner of ICT, what is actually being taught is a range of specialized subsets of what has become an all embracing generic term. What is being taught might be programming, information systems or, in our case, education. In the same way that map reading, surveying, statistics and geology might come under the collective title of geography, so these aspects come under the collective term of Information and Communications Technology. ICT being taught as a discrete subject in schools and colleges may well be transitional, a means of teaching a range of skills and applications under a flag of convenience which will disappear as staff and students become more confident in their use.

However, despite the fact that the teaching of IT in English schools was in theory a legal requirement, the use of the computer didn't always develop, especially in the primary school phase due to a lack of equipment and a lack of time and money to learn how to use the hardware and software. It was only the impetus created by the election of a Labour government in 1997 that significantly stimulated the development of ICT in both schools and teacher training colleges.

In 1996 the Parliamentary Labour Party convened a committee, under the chairmanship of Lord Dennis Stevenson, to assess the place that ICT would have in education. Many valid recommendations arose from this Report (Stevenson, 1997) which was published in March 1997, some of which have already been discussed elsewhere in this book. One of the most publicized of these was the idea that every child in British schools would have their own e-mail address by the year 2001. Although optimistic, it did nonetheless highlight the commitment that the potential new government felt towards modern technology in British schools. *Connecting the Learning Society* (DfEE, 1997a) was a document which drew directly on the recommendations of the earlier Stevenson Report and established the notion of the National Grid for Learning (NGfL). This was intended to establish an on-line community whereby all educational institutions, such as schools, museums, art galleries and libraries would be connected to the Internet and would be able to communicate by the use of e-mail. This in turn led to corresponding websites, including the Virtual Teachers Centre and the formation of the British Educational Technology Agency (BECTa) on 1 April 1998. BECTa was tasked with not only managing the content of the NGfL but also providing detailed and extensive curriculum support just as its direct predecessor the National Council for Educational Technology (NCET) had done.

Connecting the Learning Society represented the cornerstone of the new government's ICT in education policy and, as such, it had significant ramifications for teachers and teacher training institutions. DfEE *Circular 10/97* (DfEE, 1997b) established for the first time the notion of a 'National Curriculum' for initial teacher training. This was a development from *Circular 14/93*, which demanded that initial teacher training would be increasingly school rather than institution based. However, *10/97* was purely a discussion document and, although it established the idea that ICT would be an integral part of initial teacher training, at this stage it was not clearly thought through and it was decided that in the short term the requirement would be for all students to attain Level 8 of the pupils' National Curriculum for England and Wales. It was quickly appreciated, however, that the scope and content of this requirement was insufficient to meet the demands of teaching in the first part of the twenty-first century and, when the final definitive document was published in May 1998, *Teaching: High Status, High Standards – Requirements for Courses of Initial Teacher Training – Circular 4/98*, the requirements for ICT were much wider and more detailed. In Annex B of *4/98*, the requirements for ICT were divided

into two clear sections – 'Section A: Effective Teaching and Assessment Methods' and 'Section B: Trainees' Knowledge and Understanding of, and Competence with, Information and Communications Technology'. The former was concerned with learning how to use ICT to support the teaching of the core subjects of English, Mathematics and Science and the latter was concerned with the students' own ICT key skills. This placed the focus clearly on teacher training institutions to ensure that ICT was placed firmly on the curriculum and was taught in the context of the core subjects. At the same time the New Opportunities Fund made £230 million of National Lottery funding available for the training of serving teachers in English and Welsh schools in ICT. Accredited providers deliver training to a similar set of standards to those listed in Annex B of *4/98*, the idea being that by 2002 all teachers will have been trained to a similar standard.

As far as pupils in schools in England and Wales are concerned, there have been corresponding initiatives in the development of ICT which, by definition, will impact upon the courses that are offered by initial teacher training institutions. The publication in 1998 by the Qualifications and Curriculum Authority (QCA) of the *Information Technology: A Scheme of Work for Key Stages 1 and 2* at last gave schools the first officially backed structure for the teaching of ICT in British schools. Previously Local Education Authorities or, in many cases, individual schools were responsible for the production and implementation of these highly detailed and complex documents. Effectively a syllabus, it details which ICT experiences should be offered to children at certain ages during the primary phase. In a highly comprehensive document, the areas of ICT covered, with an emphasis towards literacy, include use of the Internet, multimedia authoring and presentation, e-mail, exploring simulations and combining text and graphics, writing stories, finding information, labelling and classifying and using a word bank. As a result of this non-statutory document, many schools are adopting this as a means of ensuring that there is continuity and progression throughout Key Stages 1 and 2. Laid out in tabular form, the scheme details learning objectives, possible teaching activities and learning outcomes for children in Key Stages 1 and 2. As a consequence of this, teachers in schools and the intending teachers who are going to work in those schools need to be trained to deliver the experiences detailed in the document.

The publication in late 1999 of the third version of the National Curriculum for England and Wales (DfEE, 1999), which was taught from September 2000, has also ensured that teachers need to be taught how to deliver ICT. Although a complete rewrite from its 1995 predecessor, the tone and approach of the 1999 National Curriculum is essentially similar in scope and outlook. In the introduction, 'The Importance of Information and Communication Technology', it states that

Information and communication technology (ICT) prepares pupils to participate in a rapidly changing world in which work and other activities are

increasingly transformed by access to varied and developing technology. Pupils use ICT tools to find, explore, analyse, exchange and present information responsibly, creatively and with discrimination. They learn how to employ ICT to enable rapid access to ideas and experiences from a wide range of people, communities and cultures. Increased capability in the use of ICT promotes initiative and independent learning, with pupils being able to make informed judgements about when and where to use ICT to best effect, and to consider its implications for home and work both now and in the future.

Although words such as 'find', 'explore' and 'analyse' are included once again, as they were in the 1995 Dearing version, the 1999 National Curriculum does not mention within the ICT document aspects such as ethics, values and human experience. It does, however, mention for the first time specific applications, such as e-mail and spreadsheets. The document is divided into five broad headings within the programme of study, these being: *Finding things out*; *Developing ideas and making things happen*; *Exchanging and sharing information*; *Reviewing, modifying and evaluating work as it progresses* and *Breadth of study*. It is against this background of functional key skills that courses in initial teacher training have developed.

DESIGN OF THE CURRENT COURSE

Apart from requirements for the teaching of ICT, *Circular 4/98* Annex C is also relevant. This divides the primary English curriculum into four sections: 'Section A, Pedagogical Knowledge and Understanding Required by Trainees to Secure Pupils' Progress in English'; 'Section B, Effective Teaching and Assessment Methods'; 'Section C, Trainees' Knowledge and Understanding of English' and 'Section D, Other Professional Requirements'. As with Annex B the onus is on ITT providers to look at the implications for delivery of subject programmes within ITT courses.

The way that this has been interpreted in the School of Education of Anglia Polytechnic University is to provide a core programme for all trainee teachers which contains separate compulsory modules for both English and ICT. The course has been carefully structured to integrate university teaching and school experiences whereby students complete a number of directed tasks which enable them to consolidate their learning and evidence from these tasks informs the content of the taught modules. The English modules are concerned with: *An Introduction to English in the Primary Curriculum*; *Teaching Through Texts*; *Understanding Language* and *Meeting Individual Needs*.

Initially ICT was taught in the first year only as part of a Technology module, split on a half-and-half basis with Design Technology. However, in 1998 it was realized that the importance of ICT to schools and teachers, as well as the impending requirements of *4/98*, meant that this approach was no longer acceptable as it did not provide enough contact hours or appropriate teaching and learning experiences. Two compulsory core modules of ICT were designed and delivered called *An Introduction to ICT in the Primary Curriculum* and *Effective Teaching and Assessment Methods*, one of which is taught in each of the first two years of the three-year undergraduate course. In order to ensure that there was a balance between theory and practice, the modules were taught across both semesters. This allowed the students to learn about the use of ICT in subjects at college, then go and put what they had learned into practice in school, before returning to college for reinforcement and extension prior to the next school experience. Assessment occurred at the end of the module in Semester Two and was geared towards a mixture of theory and practice, with portfolios of work providing evidence of attainment for the requirements of *4/98* as well as directed tasks designed to develop and extend professional expertise. Moreover, three additional modules were offered for those students who wished to study ICT in greater depth.

The first core ICT module introduced the students to the computer and the basic applications that could be used to support teaching and learning in all subjects in the primary curriculum, not just the core ones. This included word processing, desk-top publishing, graphics, peripherals, LOGO, databases and use of the World Wide Web. In the course of this module, the students went out on their first two school experiences. The second module explored the use of ICT to support teaching and learning, including how to evaluate educational software and how ICT could support specific subjects and areas of the primary curriculum, such as Special Educational Needs and Early Years education, which fitted around the third school experience. This arrangement was tremendously successful: along with the purchase of new hardware and software, it ensured that ICT was placed firmly on the agenda, that there was a minimum of 24 taught hours in each of the first two years of the undergraduate course and that the status of ICT was raised and consequently established in the consciousness of the students. Also, it offered the opportunity to learn and practise the use of ICT in schools in a structured and integrated way.

It is important to stress that the core ICT modules did not teach ICT skills *per se*; the necessary skills were addressed through application to the primary curriculum. Although there had to be an element of this in order to fulfil the requirements of Section B of Annex B, the focus of teaching and learning is very much towards the application of ICT to a subject context, with a particular emphasis on the core subjects of English, Mathematics and Science. Inevitably, there was overlap. As far as ICT and English were concerned, principal applications such as word processing, presentations or multimedia authoring were covered in ICT as these are generic applications that can be applied to a wide range of subjects. However, each core module for English included an ICT element which examined ICT and learning, evaluation of software for English, evaluation of websites for English, ICT in the production of written work and information retrieval and research. This approach was very successful but it meant that there had to be close co-ordination between the co-authors of this chapter in their respective roles of Head of English and ICT Co-ordinator to ensure that there were no omissions or repetition! Indeed, this issue affects all subjects. However, successful negotiation ensures that the students get a very rich and varied ICT diet and provides a good model for future curriculum development. It was against this background that the authors decided to carry out their investigation.

THE INVESTIGATION

When the investigation was undertaken at the end of 1999 all three undergraduate years had experienced both discrete ICT and English modules. The third-year students had just returned from their qualifying school experience and had completed all of their core modules, with their last semester being filled with subject specialism modules. The second-year students had completed three-quarters of their ICT and English modules and the first-year students had completed about twelve hours of each. The intention of the research was to try to assess what student perceptions were of ICT and literacy, both separately and together. Questionnaires were given to a sample of students on all three year cohorts of the primary phase three-year undergraduate initial teacher training degree course, plus those who were on the primary PGCE programme. There were 31 first-year and 37 second-year students surveyed, which represented about one third of the number of students in these cohorts, and 55 third-year students surveyed, which accounted for just under two-thirds of the year group. Additionally there were 34 PGCE students surveyed, which represented about three-quarters of that particular cohort. Each group was surveyed during practical English or ICT lectures and respondents were given the choice of whether they wished to respond or not as the figures quoted show. They were also given the option of whether or not they wanted to remain anonymous. For speed and ease of completion, questionnaires were printed on one side of A4 paper and were designed to enable respondents to give full or shorter answers as they wished. It was therefore possible for respondents to give more than one answer to each question. The questionnaires were then analysed and recorded by the authors.

Six questions were asked. These were designed to discover exactly what the students thought about both literacy and ICT, although the questions were sufficiently open-ended to elicit a wide range of interpretation. The questions were as follows:

1. What do you understand by the term literacy?
2. What do you understand by the term Information and Communications Technology (ICT)?
3. What do you think is the current role of ICT in the school curriculum?
4. What do you think is the current place of literacy in the curriculum?
5. Given the presence of new technologies, what do you think the new literacies should be?
6. What might the classroom of the future look like?

The first two questions were straightforward and were designed to discover exactly what students thought these terms meant. In order to develop courses further, it was felt that a clear definition of these key terms was essential. Questions three and four were particularly important as they clearly identified the gap between the perceived and actual roles of literacy and ICT in the curriculum. There was some expectation here that different cohorts of students would respond in different ways depending on their experience of primary schools. This is an important consideration when one remembers that the first-year and PGCE students had only been in college for a few weeks, and thus their experiences of both primary schools and teaching would, by definition, be very limited. Questions three and four were designed to elicit exactly what students thought the place of literacy and ICT was in the curriculum, whether they had a narrow perception of literacy as purely reading and writing or whether they had learned to think in somewhat broader concepts along the lines discussed in the other chapters of this book. By considering the answers to questions three and four along with question one, the authors were curious to discover whether the impact of the Literacy Hour in schools and widespread exposure in the media had affected the students' thinking. Questions five and six were designed to elicit students' perceptions of a vision of the future, to determine whether they had any clearly defined notion of what ICT and literacy might look like in the course of and at the end of their teaching careers.

The majority of the answers to question one were predictable. The bulk of the students perceived literacy as a traditional construction: 87 per cent of first years, 62 per cent of second years, 60 per cent of third years and 70 per cent of PGCE students interpreted it in this way. There may well be some correlation between the higher percentages of students who had only just begun their courses and the interpretation of literacy as reading and writing. Responses from first-year students typically included 'to be able to read and write', 'to give people the basic tool of communication', 'work involving reading, writing, speaking and listening across the National Curriculum with great importance in the subject of English' and 'being able to read fluently and confidently with a full understanding of what is being said and to be able to write in many forms'. One student had a wider interpretation stating that 'it is the study of language and knowledge through various sorts of material, such as books, media and tapes'.

The answers given by the second-year cohort were very similar in range and scope: they included responses such as 'a combination of reading, writing, speaking and listening', 'oracy, reading, writing and an understanding of language' and 'the ability to communicate and understand spoken and written language'. The third-year group viewed literacy very clearly as communication with this word appearing frequently in the questionnaires. Sample responses here included 'the art of language', 'communicating one's ideas through language' and 'communication of ideas'.

The reasons for these responses may well be because these students had received the highest number of ICT and English lectures, had spent the greatest amount of time in school and, as a result, that exposure to the 'communications message' had come through. This may possibly have been as a result of the change in terminology from Information Technology to Information and Communications Technology as well as the emphases of the new National Curriculum document and other documentation, such as *4/98* and *Connecting the Learning Society*. However, little mention was made of development of thought and understanding of development of idum. Nevertheless, one third of the students saw speaking and listening as essential elements of literacy, demonstrating an understanding of the integrated nature of language, compared to 27 per cent of second years, 22 per cent of first years and only 17 per cent of PGCE students. However, only a few students in each group saw literacy purely as grammar, comprehension and language conventions. Of a total of 157 students involved in the survey, very few made a direct link to the Literacy Hour at this point. This suggests that, although students mainly perceive literacy as reading and writing, they do not necessarily perceive literacy as a subject constrained by the objectives of the National Literacy Strategy.

Question two, which asked the students what they understood by the term ICT, received a much broader range of responses. Twelve of the first-year students saw ICT just as technology, compared to only two second years, four third years and two PGCE students. This may well have been due to the fact that at the time of the survey, some of the first years had received no ICT lectures, so may well have been relying on pre-course experiences. However, thirteen first years (42 per cent) saw it purely as electrical equipment; 35 per cent of second years, 35 per cent of third years and 17 per cent of PGCE students also perceived ICT in this way. Only 7 first years (22 per cent) and 7 second years (19 per cent) recognized the information aspect of ICT as the main focus, with 30 per cent of PGCE students and 25 per cent of third years agreeing with this. The focus of communications is also fairly consistent, with 34 per cent of first years, 43 per cent of second years, 38 per cent of third years and 29 per cent of PGCE students also seeing this as one of the main foci. Sample responses included 'all types of technology, e.g. telephones, computers', 'internet and communication to others . . . the world has become much faster and more easier', 'tools to communicate information', 'computers and the way information is passed between them', 'learning how to communicate using technology' and 'the use of computers, fax machines, calculators and other such equipment for presenting, processing and using information'. Only four students – all third years – saw ICT as a separate subject but, conversely, only fifteen students in the whole survey specifically mentioned ICT as a tool to learning! There did not seem to be a conceptual link between the place of the computer in terms of information and communication and its place as a tool to further learning.

However, in responding to the third question, which asked students for their opinion on the current role of ICT in the school curriculum, the vast majority of students *did* see ICT as a tool to learning – 71 per cent of first years, 70 per cent of second years, 62 per cent of third years but only 47 per cent of PGCE students.

However, at this point the latter group had not had any ICT lectures. That students saw ICT as a tool for learning was the response consistently across the cohorts although other aspects, such as speed and function, special needs, collaborative learning and alternative means of expression were all mentioned. These included the responses: 'to support other areas of the curriculum as well as developing ICT skills in their own right', 'to promote the use and understanding of the various new technologies which will affect all our lives', 'to allow children to become computer literate and improve presentation, learning experiences and knowledge through the use of technology', 'to support and aid the teaching of the National Curriculum subjects', 'to provide a support to learning in all subjects and give children an insight into the future', 'in the primary field to support the development of learning across the curriculum', 'to support all of the curriculum subjects' and, most interestingly of all, 'it is an integral part of the school curriculum supporting learning in other subjects, although this is not often seen in practice'. However, 22 per cent of third-year students and 38 per cent of PGCE students stated that they felt that the potential that the computer offered schools was not being met. Only two first years and four second years identified this feature so it is perhaps surprising that the PGCE group, with such limited exposure to educational ICT, should readily identify this.

Question four asked the students what they thought the current place of literacy was in the curriculum. Again, a consistent number of students across the cohorts identified literacy as a tool for learning – 42 per cent of first years, 30 per cent of second years, 33 per cent of third years and 38 per cent of PGCE students felt that this was a priority. However, the majority view was that literacy was 'high profile', with the Literacy Hour getting frequent and specific mentions. This view was shared by 62 per cent of first years, 57 per cent of second years, 78 per cent of third years and 50 per cent of PGCE students. Sample responses from the first-year students were 'the current place for literacy is very high, as children need to learn to read, write and evaluate things for themselves', 'literacy at present is seen as one of the most "important" subjects in the curriculum', 'literacy is valued highly. Literacy hour shows how the present government wish for literacy to be more important and for improvements to be made', 'top of the learning scale – it is deemed the most important as its value is greater to a child's knowledge', 'along with numeracy this has a major role – without basic understanding of literacy children could not do cross-curricular subjects'. The fact that the highest percentage of students responding in this way were third years is probably because they had had the most school experience. Sample responses included 'Literacy has greatly increased through the curriculum due to government requirements, e.g. Literacy Hour. It has taken over most of the school timetable', 'Literacy seems to be the most important part of the timetable. Schools seem to be putting all of their time and resources into this area'. Another student wrote, 'An hour of learning technical terms. No time spent on creative English.' Conversely, two students took the opposite view. One wrote, 'Very important – giving children the skills to enhance other areas of learning.' Additionally, there was a high number of mature students in this cohort, many of whom are parents of children in the primary phase. Interestingly, four of this cohort felt that the potential of literacy was not being met.

Question five was designed to explore what the students felt that literacy might involve in the future, given that new technologies would have a major impact and presence on society in general and schools in particular. Many students felt that this was a difficult concept, as 30 didn't respond to it at all, and a further 14 stated that they didn't know. This represented 28 per cent of the entire student sample. However, 25 students felt that traditional literacy skills should be part of the new literacies, and only eight felt that these skills should be replaced. There seemed to be a balance between the two. Some 45 students felt that computer literacy was the way forward, with 29 of these being in the third year. Only seven first-year students felt that there should be integration of ICT and literacy. Typical responses were 'people must be computer literate in the future', 'I think that the use of computers should be included', 'a lot will be lost if we move towards a completely technological way of learning', 'integration of computers into literacy lessons . . . less emphasis on handwriting' and 'a combination of both, the concrete as well as the abstract, like designing your own story books'. The widest range of responses came from the PGCE group, who included keyboard skills, communication, voice input, talking books and accessing information. Unsurprisingly, it was the third-year group who seemed to have the most clearly defined vision of what literacies might look like in the future. This group gave some interesting responses to this question. These included the predictable narrow interpretations such as 'talking books, input via voice to computer, internet access', 'computing and typing', 'same as always – it didn't do me any harm!', 'word processing, graphics packages, data handling packages', to broader ideas such as 'I don't think there are new literacies – just old ones adapted for new uses'. This, however, was very much a minority view.

The last question, what the classroom of the future might look like, was an attempt to elicit from the students some form of visionary response as to what their working environments might look like. Undoubtedly the overall impression from all four of the cohorts was that all children would have greater access to PCs, mainly through having their own computer on their desks. This was the majority view of the first-year cohort with a total of 26 (84 per cent) of them feeling that this was the way forward. Typical responses were 'More computers and up to date information, able to read stories on the computer, read stories from children all over the world', 'The future of classrooms may possibly be a group of computers with everything being taught from a virtual teacher (That's my job gone!), much more interactive learning through computers'. Likewise the PGCE group, also the least experienced of being in schools, leaned this way with a total of 23 students (67 per cent) agreeing with this.

The second- and third-year groups had a much wider scope of ideas, although they too felt that greater access to ICT was ultimately the likely outcome. Sample second-year responses were 'Classrooms will contain more ICT but still with a teacher, ICT is an aid to learning . . . but cannot take on all roles', 'personalised software for each pupil, with individualised learning systems', 'integrated more into the school day', 'the classroom may have more interactive learning' and, as one student put it, 'With me in it, who knows?' Overall though, this cohort were roughly divided into two equal groups – most thought that children would have greater access to computers but one group thought that technology would replace pencil and paper and the other group felt that computers would not replace traditional classroom skills. Sample third-year responses were 'conducted through one media of a computer/TV/presentation rather than a black/whiteboard and teacher', 'More ICT equipped, more of a balance between the subjects', 'If it were in line with the government's directive every child would have a laptop to record their work on'. Not all responses were optimistic though. As one student stated, 'Due to funding very similar to how they are now', while another felt that the foundation subjects would not be taught. However, two students alone in the whole survey identified the idea of distance learning as a possible vision of the future. One of the respondents said, 'Technology will work alongside other teaching tools. There will still be books and a teacher! Distance learning . . .' while the other one said, 'Digicam with the teacher at home and the children logged on from home. Like school of the air in the outback on radio.' This is a particularly interesting concept, as it provides another example of a new technology being placed in an old context, similar to the idea in Nick Easingwood's chapter on e-mail, where he likens e-mail to the telegraph communication system which appeared in old Westerns and is thus a regressive technology. Likewise, although distance learning is becoming prevalent in many universities, it too could almost be described as a regressive technology, although in this case there are visual stimuli to support the aural and oral ones of the 'School of the Air'.

Following on from this notion of where teacher and learner are located is the importance that the students gave to ICT suites. Only 4 students out of the 157 sampled mentioned that the future would involve ICT suites away from the classroom. Although this might in part be due to the phrasing of the question, there is a clear message here in that greater access to ICT equipment in their own classrooms is crucial as it will be an integral part of their everyday teaching and not divorced from it, as is the danger when children have to move to a different location. If ICT is genuinely to be a tool to learning then it needs to be in their learning environments where it is easily and instantly accessible. Sample responses were 'each class with one or more computers, all with easy access to the internet', 'it will probably have computers for every child in the class and a lot more of the lessons will be computerised learning', 'who knows?', 'hopefully more than one Acorn in the corner', 'full of PC's – all subjects will more or less involve the use of computers. All correspondence will be via e-mail'.

MAKING SENSE OF IT ALL

Although this was a relatively small-scale, preliminary research project, there are several important issues raised by the responses to the questionnaires. It provided an opportunity to assess student perceptions of a range of fundamental perceptions influencing both ICT and literacy over the next few years and in that sense it was successful. Students have clearly been influenced by the literacy message, particularly by the demands of the National Literacy Strategy from both university lectures and the need to teach the Literacy Hour during school experiences. This, of course, is little surprise but the real challenge is in getting students to perceive literacy in a wider context. However, it was encouraging in that the 'communication' message that was coming through clearly from the third-year cohort, who were just about to qualify, emphasized that a broader interpretation of literacy into a context appropriate for the twenty-first century was developing. Also encouraging was the interpretation of ICT now being about communication which was consistent across all of the cohorts surveyed, as this is an essential aspect of the use of ICT in society for the foreseeable future. The challenge for students and teachers now is in applying the same uses of ICT to the classroom as to everyday life.

The most encouraging aspect of the survey was the fact that a significant number of students perceived both literacy and ICT as tools to learning. The notion of teaching children how to learn, by providing those tools, has been a fundamental philosophical aspect of primary education since the *Plowden Report* of 1967 (HMSO, 1967) and has been given a new lease of life in *All Our Futures*. Despite the trends towards more 'formalized' elements, particularly in the primary phase, it is clear that a more flexible approach to teaching and learning is going to be essential in the future. Although many students directly linked literacy to the Literacy Hour, they also perceived the mechanics of what was being taught during these sessions as essential in equipping children with the necessary skills to survive and prosper in the twenty-first century. This was reinforced by the idea that the new literacies would consist of the use of ICT but not necessarily in the form of ICT key skills. There appeared to be a strong sense of ICT being used as a new medium to develop and adapt existing skills for a technological age, especially as many students did not think that separate ICT suites would form much of a part of future schools. The clear message was that the technology would be an integral part of everyday school life and as such would be an integral part of teaching and learning within the classroom. In other words, using technology within the teaching and learning environment would be as natural as using a pen or pencil. However, what the students omitted from their responses acted as a clear indicator as to what was missing from their knowledge and understanding. It is these gaps that particularly need to be addressed by course design as well as the importance of marrying a vision of the future with the practicalities of the present. The future is about ethics and values as much as it is about what the technology will be able to do and achieve.

COURSE REDESIGN

Having attempted to make some sense of the findings, what does this mean for the School of Education of Anglia Polytechnic University? The response was to redesign and restructure the undergraduate degree programme. ICT is no longer taught as separate, discrete modules but as an integral part of other subjects, especially the core subjects of English, Mathematics and Science, although not exclusively so. There were several reasons for this shift, not least of which was the fact that students were entering training with good ICT key skills. Although key skill development had never been a major focus under the old system, it was felt that discrete teaching was no longer necessary. Indeed, learning is not compartmentalized so, although specific applications were always taught in a subject context, it makes much more sense to teach ICT as a real, live part of a subject. A crucial response to this has been the need for the ICT co-ordinator to produce a detailed scheme of work, which has been based on the QCA scheme of work for Key Stages 1 and 2 to ensure that there are no repetitions or omissions and that there is clear continuity and progression. This needs to apply not only within subjects but also within applications. For example, it is entirely appropriate to include spreadsheets in both Science and Mathematics as the two contexts will be entirely different but from an ICT aspect it will clearly not be desirable to have identical uses of this application.

CONCLUSIONS

> If we are to prepare successfully for the twenty-first century we will have to do more than just improve literacy and numeracy skills. We need a broad, flexible and motivating education that recognises the different talents of all children and delivers excellence for everyone.

This quote, taken from the 1997 White Paper, *Excellence in Schools* (DfEE, 1997c), highlights the urgent need for the scope and purpose of the curriculum to be reconsidered. This book has challenged the traditional notion of literacy and questioned the role that it should play both now and in the future. In the Foreword Professor Stephen Heppell posed the question whether the advent of new technologies heralded the disappearance of the literate child or the beginning of an era of a newer, broader literacy. Whatever one's philosophical viewpoint, the answer has to be in favour of the latter; the literate child will exist as always and will continue to thrive, the only difference being that the nature of the literacy will have changed.

A fundamental part of interpreting and developing the understanding of the concepts that were promulgated by this book was a clear definition of what was meant by literacy. The prevailing and popular interpretation of literacy, though this might not be the intention as detailed by the National Literacy Framework, can be seen as a very formalized, narrow one involving mechanistic rules of grammar. However, the view that hopefully this book has espoused has been that the new literacies for the twenty-first century will involve the use of new technologies, not as a 'bolt-on' feature, which arguably it often is in schools now, but as an integral part of the teaching and learning that goes on in every classroom during every day of the week. If one message has come through, then it is that the new technologies can offer a great deal to education in the immediate and longer term. It is, therefore, crucially important that this opportunity is taken as this will redefine what is meant by literacy.

The early part of this chapter highlighted the main challenges that face not only serving and intending teachers but also those who have to train them. Student perceptions may be restricted by the interpretation of what, in terms of this book, might be considered a narrow definition of literacy, but that is not necessarily their fault. Messages from the media and politicians have allowed them, along with teachers and parents, to become locked into the belief that literacy corresponds to the Literacy Hour and all that entails. Given the fact that this is not a legal obligation, although it effectively accounts for a very substantial part of the overall curriculum, how can the perception of what literacy ought to consist of be changed? Re-education is necessary in order for the leap of faith to be taken that will redefine literacy for the future and take teaching and learning in our schools forward. How do we empower teachers not only to actively use the new technology which can change their teaching and the learning of their pupils fundamentally but to have the confidence in their own professional abilities to know that what they are doing is right and is of fundamental importance to their charges' future success? Assuming that we had a blank piece of paper and were asked to design a curriculum for new literacies and new technologies, what would we have to consider?

It is not only the issues arising from the questionnaires that were discussed earlier in this chapter that need to be considered. Putting aside briefly day-to-day matters such as partnership issues, other aspects such as creativity, social and cultural literacy, literacy as a tool for learning, the consequences of technologizing the world, citizenship, the challenge and the need to manage change, keeping up with change, moral and ethical issues and, possibly the most fundamental of all, the notion of the global community all need to be considered. Although some of these may be more important than others at different times, it is likely that all will need to be considered at some point. This at a time when there seems to be a great deal of concentration on literacy and numeracy, league tables and SATs results. One of the main challenges is actually getting discussion of these issues onto the agenda, never mind instigating any of them.

However, all is not lost. The DfEE document *All Our Futures: Creativity, Culture and Education*, written by the National Advisory Committee on Creative and Cultural Education and published in 1999, represents a refreshing response to the belief held by many that the concentration on 'education, education, education' involves a narrow interpretation of literacy which in turn has stifled the creativity and culture in our education system. It is a thought-provoking document and, in many ways, could well represent the 'new Plowden Report', as many of the ideas contained in it recognize the valuable philosophical issues from a previous educational generation but are framed in an upward spiral to reflect the many changes that have occurred in the intervening 30 years. Only time will tell if it has as significant an impact but it will certainly serve as a useful starting point.

One of the main messages to come through from the survey of the students discussed earlier in this chapter was the urgent need to develop and broaden the scope of their courses. Both the Foreword and the Introduction of this book specifically mentioned the role that creativity needs to have in broadening the scope of the use of ICT. Chapter 10 of *All Our Futures* specifically mentions this in the context of initial teacher training. The introduction on page 153 recognizes the fact that creativity is being hampered when it states that 'The new arrangements for initial teacher education . . . present some serious difficulties for creative and cultural education'. It goes on to say, 'If the creative potential of student teachers is ignored, it is unlikely that they will be able to promote the creative and cultural development of pupils.' This is a crucially important point. With both schools and initial teacher training establishments moving towards a concentration on testing and the attainment of standards, there is a natural concern that what education is essentially about, particularly in the primary phase, is being lost. There is also a grave danger that the demands of documents such as *4/98* will threaten the supply of specialists outside of the core areas and ICT. Furthermore, it is little surprise that schools and colleges will be strongly tempted to 'teach the tests' with the result that, at the very time when they need to be broadening the scope of their courses to meet the demands of a technological society, they are narrowing them! It is important that this issue is confronted head on. Tests and standards are not going to go away, so how can curricula be developed to allow for creativity?

One of the main points here is to separate the idea of creativity from necessarily thinking that this is entirely concerned with the arts. Creativity can be just as much a part of the core areas. As Stephen Heppell mentioned in his Foreword, it is when the computer is being used creatively that children tend to use it most constructively, most effectively and, perhaps, most prosaically, most powerfully. It is this awareness on the part of both teacher and pupil that is the key to this effective usage. However, there are of course associated problems with this. Aside from the shift in philosophy required, creative use of a computer by definition implies access to a computer, which implies a substantial investment in ICT equipment, which in turn implies a need for training to facilitate this. Point a.8 of Appendix A of *All Our Futures* states, 'According to OFSTED, the spread of attainment and differing rates of progress, both within and between schools, are wider in information technology than in any other subject . . . One in three schools in Key Stage 1 and half of all schools in Key Stages 2–4 fail to comply with statutory requirements.' It goes on to say, 'At present too few teachers are qualified to teach this subject and are expected to teach a wider range of technologies than those in which they are adequately qualified.'

In the longer term this need not be a problem. The £230 million for training under the New Opportunities Fund has already addressed this need on a national scale and Anglia Polytechnic University's move to introduce modules with ICT fully integrated into a range of subjects represents a local solution to meeting new needs. It may well take time to train the teachers and get them fully 'on message' and appreciating the philosophical aspects of what they are doing rather than just learning how to use the computer but this is crucial and the need to get across the idea that ICT is a tool to learning and no more is fundamental to the future success of curricula.

One potential problem with the current focus on core subjects is that the arts and the humanities, as well as Physical Education, are being squeezed out of an otherwise already overcrowded day. Where they are being taught, it may well be unlikely that ICT will be actively encouraged or incorporated as part of teaching and learning in those areas, as there may be a strong element of 'We don't have enough time to teach these subjects as it is, so how can we be expected to use the computer as well?' The answer, of course, is to use ICT where it genuinely enhances the teaching and learning of that subject. If it isn't giving the value added element, then it shouldn't be there. If it can provide this element, then it should be taught and if it isn't then the course as a whole isn't providing value for money. This idea isn't particularly revolutionary; *Circular 4/98* gives it official expression, when talking about appropriateness of task, as does the National Curriculum for pupils. Appendix A, point a.8 of *All Our Futures* goes on to say, 'Assessment methods must be developed which better reflect the creative element of the students' work . . . the development of team working skills is seen as invaluable by future employees . . . The introduction of project-based work at this stage would ensure that the basic grounding in information technology learnt at primary level is built on.'

This is another crucial point for course design. The term 'project work', so prevalent in the schools of England and Wales in the 1970s and 80s, is given new credence and deservedly so. Today's students and children need tomorrow's skills, both for the workplace and for society in general. If we are going to have assessments, and it seems at all levels of the education system we are, then they should reflect real, meaningful outcomes in the same way that a completed task in the 'real world' would do. People work in teams in both contexts; they may work individually on an element of a task but ultimately their contribution may be a significant element of a wider whole. This being the case they need to be able to work in a project style, often incorporating several different elements together. Learning is not compartmentalized; nor should teaching be. There has never been a greater need than now for integrated learning with ICT acting as a tool to facilitate that learning. As long ago as 1977, Kemmis *et al.* developed their conceptual framework for evaluating educational software which included a category for 'tools' software and another for 'open-ended' software. This in turn comes back to the notion that the main purpose of education is to teach children how to learn; ICT can do this by acting as a research and communication tool via e-mail, the Internet or CD-ROM, it can provide a powerful vehicle to assist single applications or it can combine applications to provide a powerful tool for learning. As this happens, every subsequent generation will find the technology easier to use than the previous one, especially as the technology is progressing at an alarmingly rapid rate. In Chapter 4 Richard Millwood has already illustrated how a technique such as video or audio editing, once the preserve of the TV, film and studio-editing professional with a suite of very expensive and highly specialized equipment, is now in the hands of the primary school child. The curriculum of the future needs to allow for this and to accept that ICT provides an opportunity to take existing models of practice and transpose them to a younger and less experienced age group. This will only increase. As time goes by the children in our schools will rapidly overtake those of a previous generation. The curricula of schools and colleges need to be flexible enough to cope with this realization, so that there is genuine continuity and progression not only within Key Stages but between them too. Those who train teachers also need to be aware of this and allow for it accordingly.

REFERENCES

DfEE (1989) *Design Technology in the National Curriculum*, London: HMSO.

DfEE (1995) *Information Technology in the National Curriculum*, London: HMSO.

DfEE (1997a) *Connecting the Learning Society*, Government Consultation Paper, London: HMSO.

DfEE (1997b) Circular 10/97: 'Teaching: high status, high standards: requirements for courses of initial teacher training'.

DfEE (1997c) *Excellence in Schools*, London: HMSO.

DfEE (1998) *The National Literacy Strategy – Framework for Teaching*, London: HMSO.

DfEE (1998) *Circular Number 4/98: Teaching: High Status, High Standards – Requirements for Courses of Initial Teacher Training*, London: HMSO.

DfEE (1999) *Information and Communications Technology in the National Curriculum 2000*, London: HMSO.

HMSO (1967) 'Children and their primary schools: A report of the Central Advisory Council for Education (England)', London: HMSO.

Kemmis, S., Atkin, R. and Wright, E. (1977) 'How do students learn?', Working papers in computer-assisted learning, **5**. Centre for Applied Research in Education, UEA.

NAACE (1999) *All Our Futures: Creativity, Culture and Education*, London: HMSO.

QCA (1998) *Information Technology: A Scheme of Work for Key Stages 1 and 2*, London: HMSO.

Stevenson, D. (1997) *Information and Communications Technology in Schools: An Independent Enquiry*. London: The Independent ICT in Schools Commission.

Index